Mindsight

Near-Death
and Out-of-Body Experiences
in the Blind

Kenneth Ring
and
Sharon Cooper

First Edition 1999

William James Center for Consciousness Studies

Library of Congress Catalog Card Number 99-60247

ISBN 0-9669630-0-8

Published by the William James Center for Consciousness Studies
at the Institute of Transpersonal Psychology
744 San Antonio Rd., Palo Alto, California 94303   (650) 493-4430

Printed in the USA by Morris Publishing
3212 E. Hwy 30, Kearney, Nebraska 68847 (800) 650-7888

This life's dim windows of the soul

Distorts the heavens from pole to pole

And leads you to believe a lie

When you see with, not through, the eye.

William Blake, *The Everlasting Gospel*

This book is dedicated to

Hugh H. Harrison

Contents

Tables

Acknowledgments

Many persons and organizations made possible this study and the report that presents our findings here. Foremost among them, however, is Hugh H. Harrison, whose support, both financial and personal, was indispensable. His deep interest in this project—as well as his wise counsel over the years—is something that has given us many occasions for gratitude. In addition, we would like to thank and acknowledge the assistance of the Institute of Noetic Sciences, which made the funding possible, in connection with which we are particularly indebted to its president, Winston (Wink) Franklin and its director of research, Marilyn Schlitz.

In carrying out the study, nothing could have been accomplished without the help of various organizations for the blind through which we were able to make contact with most of the respondents who took part in this study. Here we would like again to extend our thanks to them all: the American Council of the Blind; the American Foundation for the Blind; Blindskills, Incorporated; Massachusetts Association for the Blind; Massachusetts Commission for the Blind; the National Braille Press; the National Federation of the Blind; the National Federation of the Blind of Connecticut; Newsreel Incorporated; Theosophical Book Association for the Blind; and the Ziegler Magazine for the Blind. In addition, we need to thank our colleagues, Kimberly Clark Sharp and Bruce Greyson, each of whom brought our attention to one blind respondent whom we were able to interview for this study. Fler Beaumont was also very helpful in sending us various bibliographic materials pertaining to further cases of special interest to us. Ken Stuckey, a very knowledgeable librarian at the Perkins School for the Blind in Watertown, Massachusetts, was of enormous assistance to us in locating specialized research materials and we are also indebted to him for permitting us to use the Perkins Library and its facilities. Finally, Dr. Perry Seamonds was kind enough to serve as our ophthalmological consultant and vision specialist.

We would also like to thank Lucienne Levy who, aside from her excellent editorial work, extended herself in innumerable ways on behalf of this project. Her services to us throughout the completion of this study were invaluable.

With respect to administrative help, we would like to thank Sandra Cherry and Jane Kim for their assistance in typing some of the transcripts for this research. Most helpful of all and indeed indispensable were the labors of Deborah Nixon of the William James Center, which brought this monograph through the final stages of its production. Deborah's concern for the technical excellence and appearance of this book was deeply appreciated.

Certain colleagues were particularly helpful to us by providing detailed comments on various drafts of this book. Here we would like to single out for special thanks the following: Donal Botkin, William Braud, Gracia Fay Ellwood, Bruce Greyson, Arthur Hastings, Hugh Harrison, Lucienne Levy, Charles Tart, and Jenny Wade.

Finally, we want to return to our dedicatee, Hugh Harrison, and mention one other consideration that we would like the reader of this book to bear in mind before and during the reading of it. Hugh was drawn to an interest in this project in part because he could see that the teachings of Theosophy were very much in accord with the idea that during near-death experiences the blind should be able to see. And in that connection, Hugh (and some of his Theosophical colleagues) directed our attention to some of the pertinent literature from this body of teaching. In the end, we did not emphasize this approach in the interpretation of our data, but we would be remiss if we failed to point out here that for those who are partial to this metaphysical tradition, the findings of this study appear to be highly consistent with the conclusions leading Theosophists reached many years ago.

Foreword

Near-death experiences? Out-of-body experiences? In the blind, no less? Isn't this all rather weird?

The great writer Aldous Huxley once observed that each one of us is simultaneously the beneficiary and the victim of the culture into which we were born. We are the beneficiary, insofar as we reap the multitudinous benefits that have accrued to our culture and its accumulated knowledge, and the victim, insofar as we share the narrowness, prejudices, and pathologies of our own culture.

As modern Westerners, we are very much part of a scientifically oriented culture, and we have benefited enormously from the advances of science in so many areas of life that we can hardly start to enumerate them. The computer I write this introduction on is just one small example of what, by the standards of only a few generations ago, would seem miraculous. But, and this is an important but, we are the victims of a dominant philosophy of modern culture that sociologists long ago named "Scientism."

Essential science is a wonderful way of gaining and refining knowledge. We take an attitude of genuine curiosity toward how the universe works, we couple it with a high degree of humility and healthy skepticism about how much we already know, and discipline ourselves to constantly go to the facts, the data, to figure out the way the world is. We get the facts and then come up with theories to explain what they mean, why the world is the way it is. The scientific test of a "correct" or useful theory is that we can get new, observable results, new facts, as a result of using the theory.

It is very satisfying to come up with the theory of how

things work. Indeed, ordinary thinking often stops when we "figure things out." The discipline of science is to not stop just because your theory makes good sense to you, or seems elegant or logical, but to constantly check its logical consequences against new facts and modify it (or perhaps reject it) as necessary. I find essential science, done with the proper attitude of curiosity and humility, quite compatible with essential spirituality.

Scientism occurs when real science is stopped by the psychological process of being too satisfied with the answers we have and becoming intellectually and emotionally invested in them and attached to them. Scientism, more formally defined, is a psychological process of taking the currently accepted scientific theories about how the universe functions and subtly starting to regard them as if they were the absolute truth, beyond any further serious questioning. A theory, always subject to further test and refinement, becomes a law. Thus the process of science becomes an "ism," becomes a psychological stopping point, becomes a dogmatic belief system, like many of our most dogmatic religions.

Scientism is extremely widespread in our culture, and has an especially pervasive and pernicious influence on us because we think we're being scientific when we're actually being dogmatic and scientistic. From the viewpoint of scientism, the book by Ring and Cooper you are about to read is, at best, a mere curiosity, and more likely, a lot of nonsense! Scientism holds that the human mind is nothing but the workings of the human brain, and that any ideas about spirituality are at best an abstraction, which refers to nothing more real than abstract ideas, and are more usually examples of psychopathology, of people's refusal to accept the fact that matter is the only thing that is real, that the mind is nothing but the brain, and when the brain dies the mind dies. When followers of scientism (and, insofar as we are members of modern Western culture, we are all followers to some extent) look at near-death-experiences (NDEs), these are immediately explained away as hallucinations of a dying and pathologically functioning brain. That is all they could possibly be! The mind is nothing but a reflection of the material brain's operation according to scientism, so experiences of being out of the body, of having new kinds of vital knowledge, of being convinced that one's soul survives death, and the like must be nonsensical. (I must also note that the vehemence with which such scientistic views are often expressed constantly alerts me, as a psychologist, to the fact that there are important emotional issues here; it's not just a rational or scientific argument.)

But real science, essential science, as I indicated above, is about always being open to the facts, about always taking your own beliefs and theories lightly, about always subjecting them to further tests and never making a psychological "ism" of them. The authors of this book have practiced essential science, real science. They have looked at the facts about NDEs, particularly NDEs among the blind, and provided us with extremely stimulating and thought-provoking material that we must take into account in coming to terms with reality. Given that these facts argue strongly that there is some very real sense in which we are "spiritual" beings, not just material beings, so be it!

This brings us to what makes the material presented in this book so important. Until quite recently in human history, people in all cultures have had some kind of religious or spiritual belief system that gave them meaning, that gave them an idea of what our place in the universe was and how to live a good life in accordance with this belief. It is historically strange that, with the modern dominance of scientism, all ideas of any inherent meaning or spirituality to the universe have been declared invalid. This produces a great deal of psychological trouble in our society. My work as a psychologist, as well as the work of numerous colleagues, has convinced me that without a sense of meaning derived from something bigger than a life of personal and social gratification, human beings not only do not thrive, they sicken, and they die. The current conflict between science and religion, or, more properly, between dogmatic scientism and dogmatic religion, affects us all.

Some might feel that having some kind of spiritual belief system, something that lifts us out of the limited personal restrictions of our life, is so important that we should believe it even if science (or, more properly, scientism) seems to have shown there's no basis for a spiritual life. Yet I do not believe we can go backwards to an age of simple belief. Many of the explanations once given by religion, especially those about the material world, have been shown to be scientifically invalid. The general denial of any possible spiritual reality, however, and the active ignoring of evidence pointing toward the reality of some sort of spiritual aspect of humanity, is scientism, not science. Each of us individually, as well as our culture as a whole, must come to some kind of reconciliation between a genuinely scientific and a genuinely spiritual world view, letting go of dogmatism and psychological clinging on both sides, and embracing the facts. To slightly oversimplify the facts presented here, there is now excellent initial evidence to indicate (a) that people who are blind can have the experience of vision in their NDEs, and (b) the indication is that sometimes this is not only quite different from what we believe about the material visual system of the brain but also implies some kind of extrasensory ability, some kind of complete transcendence of the currently known limits of the material brain. These facts show us that essential scientific inquiry is opening us up to the possibility that some aspects of the spiritual are real.

The possibility that we are spiritual beings in a real way, not just a metaphorical or delusional way, is exciting and vitalizing. Given the enormous influence of scientism, and the requirements of essential science, of course, we cannot rationally embrace such a view only on the basis of the material in this book, or even of a handful of scientific studies. I suspect the response of those committed to scientism will be to ignore this book, or to nit-pick at tiny flaws that are inevitable in the beginnings of any research project. A genuinely scientific and rational response to this book will be to read it seriously and then go out and thoroughly investigate the thousands of high-quality NDE cases that are waiting to be looked at, as well as parapsychological phenomena in general. My guess is that this will further support the case that there is something real about our spiritual nature, but, as a scientist, I await with interest to see where the facts will actually take us.

As a scientist, I can assure you that this book is very important and you will have a very stimulating read. As a human being, I should say that this book will also touch your heart in important ways that are still beyond the scope of current science.

Charles T. Tart, PhD
Institute of Transpersonal Psychology
Palo Alto, California, January 1999

Authors' Note

After the completion of this book, we learned of a new case of an NDE in a congenitally blind woman whose story was, in some ways, perhaps even more remarkable than any we had discovered in the course of our own research. Although circumstances prevented our interviewing this woman, because the case itself is of such importance we elected to present it, and an account of how it came to our attention, in a special appendix. Since we were not able to investigate this case ourselves, we cannot, of course, vouch absolutely for its authenticity, but we do have the assurance of the psychologist who did conduct extensive interviews with this respondent that we need entertain no doubts on that score. We also refrain from commenting on this case or providing any interpretation of it, but we would urge the reader to compare it, in particular, with that of one of our respondents, Vicki, in respect both to its astonishing similarities as well as its striking differences. Accordingly, the reader may wish to read this appendix either in conjunction with the material presented in Chapters 3 and 4, where Vicki's NDE is extensively treated, or at the very end of the book after all the data and our conclusions have been offered.

Chapter One

Do the Blind Ever See?

The Evidence for a Paradox

There are ... reported cases where individuals who were blind because of a medically confirmed organic damage to their optical system could at the time of clinical death see the environment.... Occurrences of this kind, unlike most of the other aspects of near-death phenomena, can be subjected to objective verification. They thus represent the most convincing proof that what happens in near-death experiences is more than the hallucinatory phantasmagoria of physiologically impaired brains.

— Stanislav Grof (1)

In 1989, a well-known American physician and author introduced his then latest book with an account of a near-death experience (NDE). He told the story of a patient named Sarah who, while undergoing surgery, went into ventricular fibrillation during which time she apparently had an out-of-body experience (OBE) in which she had astonishingly clear and detailed visual perceptions of her surroundings. In any case, after she was successfully defibrillated and was able to speak again, she described to the medical team what she had been aware of when her heart had gone awry. Among other things, she had been able to discern the hairstyle of the head scrub nurse, the color of the sheets on the operating table, and even the deliciously amusing fact that the anesthesiologist who had brought her back to life was wearing mismatched socks! The attending medical team was said to be "amazed" by her uncanny and inexplicable report.

In fact, however, as we now know from more than two decades of research into NDEs, such testimony is not rare among persons who come close to death, but on the contrary is rather common. Indeed, these days, as a result of all the publicity that has been given to NDEs, probably many persons would not even be all that surprised by the incident described by this author.

The real shocker, however, lay in what the author mentioned next: "But what made Sarah's vision even more momentous was the fact that, since birth, she had been blind." (2)

Naturally, when word of this story spread, it was feasted upon by those who were keen to use it to argue for the authenticity of the NDE, and we have since seen it referred to in a number of books, articles, and letters dealing with this phenomenon.

The only problem with this intriguing episode, however, is that it is entirely false. It never happened. It was made up.

The reason we know this with certainty is that one of us (K.R.), upon first reading this book, wrote immediately to the author for further details. In reply, he rather embarrassedly confessed that he had fabricated the story on the perhaps shaky, but nevertheless (to him) justifiable, grounds that all the evidence on NDEs, and certainly the *lore* about these experiences, had convinced him that such cases, even if not yet documented, must certainly exist. (3)

For our part, we could readily understand this researcher's logic even if we couldn't support his inventive way of finding "evidence" for it. In fact, for many years now, those of us in the NDE research community, and doubtless some outside this narrow world, had been hearing rumors to the effect that indeed, during NDEs, the blind could really *see*. (4) And a number of NDE investigators, beginning with V. Krishnan (1983), recognizing the critical significance of such claims, had long ago urged that a search be made for evidence of veridical OBEs in the congenitally blind. (5)

Unfortunately, such appeals have largely gone unheeded and, though the lore that the blind can see during NDEs continues to persist (6), when one attempts to check out and track down these rumors to their source, one soon discovers that they tend to disappear into the mists of hearsay, unsubstantiated anecdote, dead ends, and, as we have seen in at least one instance, outright fabrication.

For example, a tantalizing story of apparent vision in the blind was recounted in one of Raymond Moody's books (1988). According to the author:

> On Long Island, a seventy-year-old woman who had been blind since the age of eighteen was able to describe in vivid detail what was happening around her as doctors resuscitated her after a heart attack.
>
> Not only could she describe what the instruments used looked like, but she could even describe their colors.
>
> The most amazing thing about this to me was that most of these instruments weren't even thought of fifty years ago when she could last see. On top of

all this, she was even able to tell the doctor that he was wearing a blue suit when he began the resuscitation. (pp. 134-135)

Obviously, such a tale is highly suggestive, but when one of us (K.R.) pressed Moody for details about this case, all he could remember was that he had learned of it from listening to an audio cassette provided to him by an elderly physician—but he no longer had the tape and could not recall the physician's name. (7)

In what may be an oblique reference to the same woman, however, we have this allusive commentary from a television journalist: (8)

Another NDE we tried to record had offered an unusual verification. An eminent American researcher said an elderly woman, blind since she was a young girl, was able to see again when out-of-body during an NDE. In this 'sighted' state she correctly described the goings-on about her. Unfortunately, she was not interested in taking part in our television programme. (9)

Another intriguing case was furnished by the noted thanatologist, Elisabeth Kubler-Ross. In one version, a well-known journalist gave this account of it:

Dr. Kubler-Ross showed me a remarkable report involving a research chemist who had been blinded a year earlier in a laboratory experiment. Despite his blindness, during a subsequent near-death experience, he was able to view everything that went on around him and report accurately what he had seen after he was revived. (10)

Like the story of the apocryphal Sarah, this one too has since been retold in various publications (11), but Kubler-Ross herself never provided further details about it, much less any documentation of her claim.

In some of her books, however, Kubler-Ross does herself make mention of her research on blind patients, but even here she merely reports in general terms what she has found and offers little more than an avowal that the blind can really see. For instance, in her book, *On Children and Death* (1983), she asserts that during NDEs:

> ...blind people could see. We, naturally, checked these facts out by testing patients who had been blind with no light perception for years. To our amazement, they were able to describe the color and design of clothing and jewelry the people present wore. (p. 208)

Yet, to our disappointment, we find there are no specifics given concerning the nature of these tests, the controls that were exercised in making them, the protocols from the patients, or any other details that would allow for an evaluation of these extraordinary claims. Kubler-Ross and her colleagues may have been "amazed" at what they discovered, but the rest of us, no pun intended, are essentially left in the dark as a result of her failure to provide any documentation.

Other researchers have voiced much the same criticism of Kubler-Ross for her failure to back up in a scientific way her oft-mentioned declarations regarding apparent sight in the blind. Ian Wilson, the English author, for example, cites this more ample quotation from one of Kubler-Ross' lectures as a dubious case in point:

> We asked them [blind patients] to share with us

what it was like when they had this near-death experience. If it was just a dream fulfillment, those people would not be able to share with us the color of the sweater worn, the design of a tie, or minute details of shape, color and design of people's clothing. We have questioned several totally blind people who were able to share with us in [sic] their near-death experience and they were not only able to tell us who came into the room first, and who worked on the resuscitation, but they were able to give minute details of the attire and the clothing of all the people present, something a totally blind person would never be able to do. (12)

Wilson (1987) then comments, rather acerbically:

Regrettably, Dr. Kubler-Ross has tended to be too committed to her patients to spend time publishing these cases in the proper depth to prove her point. It would have been helpful to be told, for instance, whether some or all of these people had been blind since birth; one can only assume not, since anyone blind since birth would need to learn the recognition of colors (pp. 130-131).

A similar frustrating lacuna was present in the research of another pioneer NDE investigator, Dr. Fred Schoonmaker (Audette, 1979) of Denver's St. Luke Hospital, whose work was first described in an issue of a newsletter of an NDE organization. In a telephone conversation with one of us (K.R.) in 1981, Schoonmaker referred to the NDEs of three of his patients who were blind and specifically mentioned that one of them, a congenitally blind woman, was able to see the members of the medical team and could describe some of the medical procedures to which she was subjected, although she was not able to distinguish colors. Although exhorted to publish a report of this astonishing case and his observations on his other sightless patients, Dr. Schoonmaker never did so. Thus, once again, we are left with another provocative but ultimately unsubstantiated anecdote of the sort that promotes the lore that the blind can see during their NDEs. Without documentation, of course, there is no way that it can be regarded as evidential.

Still other exemplars of this species of beguiling testimony can be garnered from the annals of war veterans who have been blinded in combat. One such case, kindly furnished to us by a correspondent in New Zealand (13) concerns one Gilbert Nobbs, an English officer of the Rifle Brigade, who lost his sight permanently in battle during the First World War in September, 1916. In 1939, he published an article (Nobbs, 1939) about this episode in which it is clear that he had an NDE—*and* that, according to him, he was able to see. In his account, he describes the familiar feelings of peace and "an indescribable happiness," and other features of NDEs, but what is pertinent to us here is his claim that at one point, "I seemed for a moment somewhere in the emptiness, looking down at my body lying in the shell-hole, bleeding from the temple. I was dead, and that was my body; but I was happy!" (p. 787)

Another case of apparent visual perception in the blind—and the only one in this set where there is a measure of documentation provided by interview protocols and medical records—comes from an American veteran of the Vietnam War who was almost fatally wounded in a mine explosion on May 29, 1969. In this accident, the soldier lost both legs and an arm—as well as his sight, albeit only for a period of three weeks. Some years later, he was interviewed by the pioneer NDE researcher, Michael Sabom, a cardiologist, and his case was subsequently presented in Sabom's book, *Recollections of Death* (1982).

His NDE began to unfold while he still lay unconscious just after the explosion, but continued when he was undergoing surgery. With respect to his perceptions during these times, here are some relevant excerpts from his interview with Sabom (1982):

> When I came down and hit the ground, I remember sitting up and I saw my right arm gone and my right leg gone and my left leg was laying off to the left side. I fell back and I remember that very clearly.... I'm laying there on the battlefield and I came out of my body and I perceived me laying on the ground with three limbs gone. I knew it was me. I recognized me. (pp. 72-3)

> [Later, while in surgery] The whole time I'm looking at my body it was always from the upper left.... They picked me up and run me in [to the operating room].... I remember them sticking a tube down my mouth—the air tube or anesthesia tube or whatever.... At the beginning [of the operation] I saw them cut my uniform off and start whatever fluid they have to start. At that time my left leg was cut off. It was only hanging by a piece of skin.... I saw them cut the rest of it off.... Most of the perception was in sight, if that's what it's called. (pp. 167-8)

As to the status and possibility of his physical vision at the time, the soldier went on to tell Sabom:

> I had no eyesight for about three weeks. I literally

could not open my eyes. I had bandages on them to start with. They had been singed and burned. (p. 73)

This case obviously furnishes some compelling evidence in support of the hypothesis that the blind can see during their NDEs, but even it is not absolutely conclusive. For one thing, the soldier's blindness was by his own admission only temporary and, for another, a reading of the excerpts from the medical records that Sabom cites makes no mention whatever of the patient's alleged blindness.

This, then, is the sort of largely anecdotal data that continues to fuel the flames of belief that the blind can indeed sometimes see when they are close to death. Clearly, however, the question of whether the blind can *actually* see during their NDEs is still a vexed one. Some of the stories we have considered are certainly intriguing, but as a body of research findings, it is plain the evidence is not going to persuade any critical thinker of anything more than the remote possibility that this paradoxical assertion *might be* true. Some commentators who have looked into this matter are even less charitable. For instance, Susan Blackmore, the English parapsychologist, in her book *Dying to Live* (1993) reviewed the kind of reports we have examined here and concluded that *none of it* holds up to scrutiny. In her opinion, there is no convincing evidence of visual perception in the blind during NDEs, much less documented support for *veridical* perception.

Nevertheless, while there is every reason to concur with Blackmore's assessment, there is at least one research study that did attempt to inquire whether any evidence for this proposition could be gathered by systematically interviewing a sample of blind respondents. Credit for this pioneering venture goes to an Australian parapsychologist, Harvey Irwin, who has had a long-standing interest in near-death and out-of-body experiences. In 1987, he reported the results of an investigation in which he had field workers survey a sample of twenty-one blind persons in Australia (14). The focus of Irwin's project was to see whether any such persons had had an OBE and, if so, to get an account of it.

In his set of twenty-one respondents, three persons did indeed report having had an OBE. Unfortunately, as Irwin ruefully had to admit, all of these persons had either some residual or peripheral vision, so they did not in the end constitute anything like a stringent cohort in terms of which to evaluate the hypothesis that the blind can see. Irwin's own conclusion at the time was that neither his own survey nor the work of anyone else had demonstrated that persons blind from birth even have OBEs, (15) and therefore no evidence existed that such individuals could see under such circumstances. "It now remains," he said, "for further surveys to locate an OBE in a congenitally totally blind person" (Irwin, 1987, p. 57). This is precisely what we have attempted to do in this study and, to anticipate our findings, what we have succeeded in doing.

In short, in the remainder of this book, we wish to describe the results of a research project in which an effort was made to locate and interview blind persons, including those blind from birth, who believed they had undergone either an NDE, or an OBE not related to any near-death incident. The principal underlying aim of this study, however, will already be apparent: We were concerned to determine, whether *in fact* any reliable evidence could be educed from such a sample that the blind really *do* see under such conditions.

The significance of such findings, should they be established, has largely been implicit in this discussion thus far, so let us take a moment to lay out some of the critical issues involved here. The first of these is whether someone blind from birth can have visual experience comparable to that of a sighted person when undergoing either an NDE or OBE. Evidence for this would obviously challenge the nearly universal assumption that seeing involves a process of learning and requires an intact visual system. Thus, such findings would raise profound questions about mind-body relationships, the role of the brain in vision and indeed the very mechanisms of sight. Furthermore, empirical support for sight in the blind would be consistent with various "New Paradigm" conceptions of science that are rooted in non-local, non-dual or holonomic perspectives in which consciousness is taken to be the primary reality.

The second issue, which the first suggests but does not necessarily logically entail, is whether there is psi functioning in the blind under these conditions. If it could be shown, for instance, that blind respondents, in the absence of relevant sensory cues or other information available by normal means, can detect and accurately report visual aspects of their physical environment, it would be difficult to deny some kind of paranormal processing here.

Another issue that our inquiry may illuminate is one that has been the more immediate concern of parapsychologists, viz., the nature of the OBE itself and the basis of the vision that is said to occur during such episodes. For example, Krishnan has argued that the perceptions reported during OBEs may have a physical basis. As a test of this hypothesis, Krishnan (1983) has proposed that the OBEs of congenitally blind persons should be distinct from those with sight. Irwin (1987), in his discussion of this issue frames the implications neatly:

> Specifically, because people who surgically regain their sight take some time to learn visual identification of objects, the initial OBEs in the congenitally blind should exhibit the same property

> if the experience depends upon the visual pathways
> of the nervous system. The content of a
> congenitally blind subject's OBE therefore may
> speak to Krishnan's notion of the physical basis of
> out-of-body visual impressions. (p. 54)

Our data will thus provide a crucial test of Krishnan's
hypothesis, as well as speak to the long-standing
controversy in parapsychology over whether the OBE
represents some kind of true extrasomatic state or only a
retrospective reconstruction based on sensory cues and
imaginal processes (e.g., Blackmore, 1993).

In any case, the possible epistemological and even
metaphysical implications of our findings are no mere
trifles, but potentially touch on deep conundrums and
perennial concerns in the history of both normal and anti-
establishment science. At the same time, the reader should
be advised that the exploration of this apparent paradox of
seeing in the blind is fraught with many perplexing
ambiguities, such as the meaning of "sight" to persons who
have no history or experience of vision. Thus, questions
that appear straightforward in the asking may not
necessarily resolve themselves into definitive answers. All
this, however, is merely to anticipate some of the
complexities involved in this study, which will be
addressed at length in our final interpretative chapter.

At the moment, of course, we are far from these
considerations. Instead, we must return to the specific and
limited objectives of this inquiry, of which there are three
that served as foci for this investigation. Each can be
phrased as a question.

First, because we were chiefly interested in NDEs
in this research, there is a necessary preliminary question
we need to answer to which no previous systematic
investigation has even been addressed. That question is: Do

blind persons in fact have NDEs and, if they do, are the NDEs the same as or different from those of sighted persons?

Second, do blind persons, if they do report either NDEs or OBEs, claim to have visual perceptions during these experiences?

And, finally, if such claims are made, is it ever possible to corroborate them through independent evidence or the testimony of other witnesses? In other words, can one establish that these claims are something other than mere fantasies or hallucinations?

These were the issues, then, this study was designed to probe. The next chapter describes how we went about gathering our evidence.

Chapter Two

The Study

Procedure and Sample

In order to recruit qualified participants for this research project, that is, blind persons who believed they had had either an NDE or an OBE, we first made contact with eleven American organizations for the blind, including national, regional, and state associations, to solicit their help in locating potential respondents among their membership. Toward this end, we provided a notice to these organizations about our research that was then included in their respective publications, most of which were distributed in Braille or in the form of an audio cassette. In this notice we provided our phone number and address and simply invited interested individuals, who believed they were qualified to take part in this study, to call or write us. A similar announcement was also published in *Vital Signs,* the newsletter of the American branch of the International Association for Near-Death Studies. Finally, we alerted a few of our colleagues in the field of near-death studies about our project and asked them to refer any potentially eligible candidates to us.

After an individual made contact with us, we conducted a screening interview over the telephone to make sure that the person had the appropriate qualifications for our study. Specifically, we determined the sight status of the person and made sure that he or she had undergone either an NDE or one or more OBEs. For the purposes of this study, an NDE was defined as any type of conscious experience associated with a condition that was unquestionably life-threatening (such as a serious accident, illness, suicide attempt, or a surgical intervention that resulted in a near-death crisis), regardless of whether it conformed to the familiar classic pattern of the Moody-type NDE. An OBE on the other hand was defined here as an experience, *not* associated with a near-death condition, in which the individual finds himself or herself to be separated from his or her physical body leading to the subjective conviction that the locus of the perceiving self has become exteriorized.

Once the person's eligibility for the study was established, we either then continued with the formal interview or scheduled a second call for that purpose. (In a few cases, one or more follow-up calls were necessary to clarify some aspects of the respondent's account.) In the interview, we took a detailed sight history from the individual and then conducted an in-depth probe about his or her relevant experience(s). This portion of the interview was modeled on the format originally devised by Ring (1980), but was tailored to the specific interests of this study and the special characteristics of our respondents. In the course of this interview, however, particular attention was given to obtaining information about events or perceptions that in principle could be corroborated by external witnesses or medical records. Where those witnesses could be specifically identified or relevant records secured, we made efforts to gain access to them and, when possible, to interview the witnesses about their own recollections of the events or perceptions described by the respondent.

All conversations were tape recorded with the permission of the respondent and transcripts based on these conversations were later prepared to permit detailed analysis of our findings. Finally, each participant who expressed an interest to receive information about the findings of this study was sent a summary at its conclusion.

Of the 46 persons who were screened for this study, a total of 31 qualified for inclusion and were interviewed. All but three of this final sample had heard about our study through the notices we had distributed. The exceptions were two persons referred to us by professional colleagues and one individual who came fortuitously to the attention of one of us as a result of meeting her husband while traveling to a professional conference.

Demographically, our sample consisted of 20 females and 11 males whose ages ranged from 22 to 70. They were all Caucasian, overwhelmingly Christian with respect to their original religious tradition, but varied greatly regarding their educational attainment and occupation.

Experiential status. Sixteen of our respondents had survived an NDE, while an additional five persons had undergone both an NDE and one or more OBEs on other occasions not associated with their near-death incident. Thus, the total number of near-death experiencers (NDErs) in this sample is twenty-one. The remainder, ten, are persons who had one or more OBEs only.

Of our NDErs, thirteen had their experience in connection with an illness or a surgical procedure, six as a result of an accident (usually involving an automobile), two were mugged, one was nearly killed by being raped, one almost perished in combat, and one survived a suicide attempt. (The totals here are twenty-four since three persons had two separate NDEs each and were therefore counted twice.)

Most of the OBEs reported occurred during states of bodily quiescence or relaxation, though some were occasioned by traumas, such as falls or rapes. The great majority of these episodes were not deliberately induced, though a few persons in our sample did claim to be able to bring them about on occasion through an act of will.

Sight status. Not quite half of our total sample, fourteen, was composed of persons blind from birth. (16) An additional eleven persons fell into the category of adventitiously blind, which means they lost their sight sometime after five years of age. The remaining six persons in our study were individuals who were severely visually impaired, most of them having at best only minimal non-delineated vision. (17)

With respect to our two main experiential categories, NDEs and OBEs, the breakdown on sight status is shown in Table 1.

Table 1

Sight Status of Respondents

Sight Status	NDErs	OBErs	Total
Blind from birth	10	4	14
Adventitiously blind	9	2	11
Severely visually impaired	2	4	6

Of the fourteen respondents blind from birth, only three were full term births. The remaining eleven were born prematurely between 1946 and 1958 and all were placed in incubators where they received excessive concentrations of oxygen resulting in blindness. These individuals developed retrolental fibroplasia (RLF), now commonly referred to as retinopathy of prematurity (ROP).

Of our eleven adventitiously blind respondents, seven lost their vision between the ages of sixteen and forty-one as a result of illness or accident. In some cases, it was their near-death event itself that caused their blindness. The other four lost their vision between the ages of thirteen and fifty-two due to slow degenerative eye diseases including retinitis pigmentosa (RP), glaucoma, and aging.

Three of our six visually impaired respondents developed RLF, two had RP, both of whom had limited peripheral vision (fourteen and twenty degree field, respectively), and one was born with cataracts and developed glaucoma as a teenager. All six have been legally blind from birth (18) and only three of these individuals have been able to read any print at all.

Chapter Three

NDEs in the Blind

Obviously, before we can explore the question whether or in what sense the blind may see during NDEs, we must first establish that such persons do indeed *have* NDEs and, if they do, whether they are similar to or different from those that have been reported by sighted individuals. To examine this issue, we must of course restrict ourselves to the twenty-one respondents in our sample, twelve women and nine men, who define our NDE sample. As indicated earlier, of these, ten were blind from birth, nine were adventitiously blind, and two were classified as severely visually impaired.

As we will demonstrate shortly, our findings with respect to these initial questions are unequivocal: *The blind persons in our sample, even those blind from birth, recount experiences that clearly conform to the familiar prototype of the beatific NDE first popularized in Raymond Moody's book,* Life After Life *(1975).* Their narratives, in fact, tend to be indistinguishable from those of sighted persons with respect to the elements that serve to define the classic NDE pattern, such as the feelings of great peace and well-being that attend the experience, the sense of separation from the physical body, the experience of traveling through a tunnel or dark space, the encounter with the light, the life review, and so forth. In short, the story blind persons tell of their journey into the first stages of death is the common story we have come to associate with these episodes.

Before we turn to a statistical summary of our findings, however, it will be helpful to present a few illustrative cases in order to provide a sense of the actual narrative texture of these experiences. In doing so, we will unavoidably discover some unmistakable evidence pertaining to our second, but primary, question, having to do with whether the blind *see* during their NDEs. Nevertheless, we must defer a detailed consideration of this issue for the time being since our purpose here is chiefly to report what some of our respondents told us they remembered when they found themselves hovering between life and death.

Case 1: Vicki Umipeg (19)

Vicki Umipeg is a married forty-three-year-old woman, living in Washington State, who has had two near-death experiences. The first, when she was twelve years old, occurred on February 12, 1963, as a result of appendicitis and peritonitis. Her second NDE took place almost exactly a decade later, on the night of February 2, 1973, when she was seriously injured in an automobile accident.

Vicki was born very prematurely, having been in the womb only twenty-two weeks at delivery, and weighed just three pounds at birth. (Afterward, however, her weight dropped precariously to one pound, fourteen ounces.) As was common for premature babies in the mid-twentieth century, she was placed in a then new airlock incubator through which oxygen was administered. Unfortunately, because of a failure to properly regulate the concentration of oxygen, Vicki was given too much and—along with about 50,000 other premature babies born in the United States about the same time—suffered such optic nerve damage as to leave her completely blind. As she makes clear in an initial interview with another researcher, Greg Wilson, (20) who kindly provided his tapes and transcripts to us, she has never had any visual experience whatever nor does she even understand the nature of light.

> Interviewer: Could you see anything?
> Vicki: Nothing, never. No light, no shadows, no nothing, ever.
> Interviewer: So the optic nerve was destroyed to both eyes.
> Vicki: Yes, and so I've never been able to understand even the concept of light.

Interestingly, the overall form of Vicki's two experiences, which were separated by a period of ten years, is extremely similar, almost as though they were replays of one another, albeit with some variations owing to the particularities of Vicki's life circumstances on each occasion. To minimize redundancy, we will present a fairly full exposition here only of Vicki's second NDE, when she was twenty-two years old, since according to her own testimony, it was the more detailed and vivid of the two. However, to lay the groundwork for subsequent discussion, it should be noted here that throughout *each* of her experiences, she reports being able to see things of this world, however briefly, as well as otherworldly visions. In addition, both her childhood and adult NDE feature a complete panoramic life review during which she also claims to have been able to see significant persons and events of her life. Here, then, is an account of Vicki's second NDE.

In early 1973, Vicki, then twenty-two, was working as an occasional singer in a night club in Seattle. One night, at closing time, she was unable to call for a taxi to drive her home and circumstances forced her to take the only other option, to ride in a Volkswagen bus with a couple of patrons both of whom were inebriated. Not surprisingly, a serious accident ensued during which Vicki was thrown out of the van. Her injuries were extensive and life-threatening, and included a skull fracture and concussion, and damage to her neck, back, and one leg. (In fact, it took her a full year after being released from the hospital before she could stand upright without the risk of fainting.)

Vicki clearly remembers the frightening prelude to the crash itself, but she has only a hazy recall of finding herself alternately out of her body and then back inside of it at the accident scene. Her only definite recollection of anything external to herself while out-of-body is a very brief glimpse of the crumpled VW bus. Although this aspect of her experience was confusing, she does claim to have been aware at the time that while in her out-of-body state she did find herself in a non-physical body that had a distinct form and that "was," as she put it, "like it was made of light."

She has no memory of the her trip to Harborview Hospital in the ambulance, but after she arrived at the hospital's emergency room, she came again to awareness when she found herself up on the ceiling watching a male doctor and a woman (she is not sure if the woman was another physician or a nurse) working on her body. She could overhear their conversation too, which had to do with their fear that because of possible damage to Vicki's eardrum, she could become deaf as well as blind. Vicki tried desperately to communicate to them that she was fine, but naturally drew no response. She was also aware of seeing her body below her, which she recognized by certain establishing identity features (to be further discussed later in this section).

What, exactly, did Vicki claim to see? According to

her testimony, she first had a very fleeting image of herself lying on the metal table and she was sure, she said, that "it was me," although it took her a moment to register that fact with certainty. As she later told us:

> I knew it was me.... I was pretty thin then. I was quite tall and thin at that point. And I recognized at first that it was a body, but I didn't even know that it was mine initially. Then I perceived that I was up on the ceiling, and I thought, "Well, that's kind of weird. What am I doing up here?" I thought, "Well, this must be me. Am I dead?..." I just briefly saw this body, and ... I knew that it was mine because I wasn't in mine. Then I was just away from it. It was that quick.

Almost immediately after that, as she recalls, she found herself going up through the ceilings of the hospital until she was above the roof of the building itself, during which time she had a brief panoramic view of her surroundings. She felt very exhilarated during this ascension and enjoyed tremendously the freedom of movement she was experiencing. She also began to hear sublimely beautiful and exquisitely harmonious music akin to the sound of wind chimes.

With scarcely a noticeable transition, she then discovered she had been sucked headfirst into a tube and felt that she was being pulled up into it. The enclosure itself was dark, Vicki said, yet she was aware that she was moving toward light. As she reached the opening of the tube, the music that she had heard earlier seemed to be transformed into hymns (similar to those she heard during her '63 NDE), and she then "rolled out" to find herself lying on grass.

She was surrounded by trees and flowers and a vast

number of people. She was in a place of tremendous light, and the light, Vicki said, was something you could feel as well as see. Even the people she saw were bright.

> Everybody there was made of light. And I was made of light. What the light conveyed was love. There was love everywhere. It was like love came from the grass, love came from the birds, love came from the trees.

Vicki then becomes aware of specific persons she knew in life who are welcoming her to this place. There are five of them. Debby and Diane were Vicki's blind schoolmates, who had died years before, at ages eleven and six, respectively. In life, they had both been profoundly retarded as well as blind, but here they appeared bright and beautiful, healthy and vitally alive. They were no longer children, but, as Vicki phrased it, "in their prime." In addition, Vicki reports seeing two of her childhood caretakers, a couple named Mr. and Mrs. Zilk, both of whom had also previously died. Finally, there was Vicki's grandmother—who had essentially raised Vicki and who had died just two years before this incident. Her grandmother, however, who was further back than the others, was reaching out to hug Vicki. In these encounters, no actual words were exchanged, Vicki says, but only feelings—feelings of love and welcome.

In the midst of this rapture, Vicki is suddenly overcome with a sense of total knowledge:

> I had a feeling like I knew everything ... and like everything made sense. I just knew that this was where ... this place was where I would find the answers to all the questions about life, and about the planets, and about God, and about everything....

It's like the place was the knowing.

And then she is indeed flooded with information of a religious nature as well as scientific and mathematical knowledge. She comes to understand languages she doesn't know. All this overwhelms and astonishes her:

> I don't know beans about math and science.... I all of a sudden understood intuitively almost things about calculus, and about the way planets were made. And I don't know anything about that.... I felt there was nothing I didn't know.

As these revelations are unfolding, Vicki notices that now next to her is a figure whose radiance is far greater than the illumination of any of the persons she has so far encountered. Immediately, she recognizes this being to be Jesus (for she had seen him once before, during her '63 NDE). He greets her tenderly, while she conveys her excitement to him about her newfound omniscience and her joy at being there and with him again.

Telepathically, he communicates to her: "Isn't it wonderful? Everything is beautiful here, and it fits together. And you'll find that. But you can't stay here now. It's not your time to be here yet and you have to go back."

Vicki reacts, understandably enough, with extreme disappointment and protests vehemently, "No, I want to stay with you." But the being reassures her that she will come back, but for now, she "has to go back and learn and teach more about loving and forgiving."

Still resistant, however, Vicki then learns that she also needs to go back to have her children. With that Vicki, who was then childless but who "desperately wanted" to have children (and who has since given birth to three), becomes almost eager to return and finally consents.

However, before Vicki can leave, the being says to her, in these exact words, "But first, watch this."

And what Vicki then sees is "everything from my birth" in a complete panoramic review of her life, and as she watches, the being gently comments to help her understand the significance of her actions and their repercussions.

The last thing Vicki remembers, once the life review has been completed, are the words, "You have to leave now." She then experiences "a sickening thud" like a roller-coaster going backwards and finds herself back in her body, feeling heavy and full of pain.

Case 2: Brad Barrows

Brad Barrows is a thirty-three-year-old man, living in Connecticut, who had a near-death experience in the winter of 1968 when he was only eight years old. At the time, he was a student at the Boston Center for Blind Children, and had contracted a severe case of pneumonia.

Like Vicki, Brad has been completely blind from birth, though not for the same reasons. Although he was born two weeks premature, that appears to have had nothing to do with his blindness. As Brad explained it to us:

> My eyes never developed correctly and, basically, the tissue in my eyes is not very well-delineated. I do have eyes but the tissue inside is very randomly placed. I don't even have a clear eye color—they kind of look opaque white.... [As a result] I've been blind since birth. I have never been able to see in my life.... Everything else in

my body was completely normal: brain scan, EKGs, and so the only thing the doctors could figure out at the time was that my eyes didn't develop correctly, and it was just a quirky medical fact.

A summary of his NDE follows:

In February, 1968, while at the Boston Center for Blind Children, Brad remembers that for a week before his NDE, he had been feeling very weak and tired. He was also having a difficult time breathing, but simply assumed he had a cold and did not seek any medical treatment for his condition. However, he continued to have breathing difficulties, preventing him from sleeping well, and eventually developed a fever. One night, when he was particularly feverish,

> Somewhere in the middle of the night, I began to become very stiff and rigid, and I was gasping for air. I wondered why I was having so much trouble breathing. It was becoming for me very frightening and very dangerous. I really thought I was about to die.... I remember that my breathing had virtually stopped. I couldn't get any breath at all.

It was at this moment that Brad's NDE proper commenced, as he became aware that he was slowly lifting up from the bed. "It was," he said, "as if my being was slowly floating up through the room." He remembers, when he was close to the ceiling, seeing his apparently lifeless body on the bed. He also saw his blind roommate get up from his bed and leave the room to get help. (His roommate later confirmed this, Brad said.)

Next, he found that he was able to penetrate the second floor ceiling of his room and, like Vicki, soon found that he "was going straight up toward the roof of the building, actually up and over it." As in Vicki's case, this upward movement was very rapid. But once he had emerged from the building, he discovered that he could see quite clearly.

Brad estimates that it was between 6:30 and 7 o'clock in the morning when this happened. He noticed that the sky was cloudy and dark. There had been a snowstorm the day before, and Brad could see snow everywhere except for the streets that had been plowed, though they were still slushy. Brad could also observe the snow banks that the plows had created. He saw a street car go by. Finally, he recognized a playground used by the children of his school and a particular hill he used to climb nearby.

When asked if he "knew or saw" these things, he said, "I clearly visualized them. I could suddenly notice them and see them.... I remember ... being able to see quite clearly."

At this point, in almost exact parallel with Vicki, Brad was aware of being pulled at perhaps a 45-degree angle upward into a dark tunnel and at the same time hearing a noise that reminded him of the hum of an electric transformer, which at first he found somewhat irritating and even momentarily frightening. In Brad's case, the tunnel became increasingly narrow and confining for a time, but then it widened, and as the noise faded, Brad "felt as if I might be entering another realm altogether, an unexplained dimension that I had very little understanding of."

As he approached the end of the tunnel, he was aware of an "immense field" stretching before him for what seemed like miles. As he took in this scene, he says "I knew that somehow I could sense and literally see everything that was around me." He noticed, for example, huge palm trees, with enormous leaves, and very tall grass as well.

Brad was now walking on a path in this field and was overcome by the beauty of his surroundings and the feeling of homecoming it engendered in him. His description of this environment and his ecstatic condition when experiencing it is well worth quoting at length:

> When I noticed that I was walking up this field, it seemed as if I was so exhilarated and so unbelievably renewed ... that I ... didn't want to leave. I wanted to stay forever where I was. The only way I could describe it adequately would be that it was a feeling that I had as if I were home, and I didn't want to leave.... It was so unbelievably peaceful that there [is] no way that I could describe the peace and the tranquillity and the calm.... [The] weather was absolutely perfect in terms of temperature and humidity. It was so fresh, so unbelievably fresh that mountain air on earth could not even come close.... It was absolutely refreshing, wonderfully refreshing.
>
> The other thing I noticed was that I knew there was something beyond the senses that I'd ever had on earth that told me there was tremendous light up there. It seemed to come from every direction.... It was all around and everywhere that I happened to be looking.... I recall that vividly.

Although Brad was glorying in these sensations and feelings, he was initially somewhat puzzled by his apparent ability to see in this realm ("At first, I was taken aback by it. I did not understand what sensation I was experiencing."), but soon found it completely natural. Again, in connection with his awareness of the all-pervasive light, he makes these instructive comments:

> It seemed to be all-encompassing. It seemed like everything, even the grass I had been stepping on seemed to soak in that light. It seemed like the light could actually penetrate through everything that was there, even the leaves on the trees. There was no shade, there was no need for shade. The light was actually all-encompassing.

> Yet I wondered how I could know that because I had never seen before that point. At first I was taken aback by it. I did not understand what sensation I was experiencing. While I was moving through this particular field, I seemed to accept it very readily. I felt like I wouldn't understand it had it happened ... on earth. But where I was, I was able to accept it almost immediately.

As his experience progressed, Brad now became aware of what he felt were "many, many thousands of human voices." Again in this respect, this feature mirrors what Vicki had reported. In Brad's words:

> I remember thinking that the voices seemed to be singing in a language I had never understood or maybe many, many languages. The music I had heard was nothing like anything I have ever experienced on earth.... The rhythms were extremely thrilling and very gentle, almost like you hear in New Age music.

As he draws closer to the music, he becomes increasingly fascinated with it and wants to add his own voice to it. He senses he is on the verge of something tremendous, that he is about to meet God. "And I wanted to see this being. I wanted to be with him forever."

What happens next, however, is that Brad finds himself coming to a glittering massive stone structure which itself seems to be made of light. At first, he is afraid that the light emanating from this marvelous edifice will burn him if he approaches it, but he finds that is not the case and enters it. He discovers that he is walking within a huge tubular environment where he again hears the music which seems to be praising God. As he is advancing toward the music, suddenly a large and firm arm reaches out and stops him in his tracks. Brad doesn't know who this being is, but says he felt very comfortable with him and no sense of threat. On the contrary, "I felt a presence of tremendous love around this being." He goes on to say about his encounter that:

> What was interesting was that he did not have to say a single word to me. It was almost as if he planted a thought in my mind. The thought kind of went to the effect that I needed to come back to the earth because I was not ready for this plane yet.

Brad still does not want to return, but he now knows he must. The last thing he is aware of, before he leaves this realm, is the being gently nudging him back, which initiates a reverse movement, at lightning speed, catapulting him through the tube, across the field, and into the tunnel again whereupon he wakes up to find himself in bed gasping for air with a rectal thermometer in his buttocks. Later, he learned from a nurse that his heart had indeed stopped for four minutes, along with his breathing, and that only CPR had brought him back from death. The sudden resumption of his heartbeat, he believes, was responsible for the rapidity of his return to his body.

Case 3: Marsha

Marsha is a forty-year-old married woman living in Connecticut who had an NDE on January 16, 1986, when she was 32, as a result of complications in her pregnancy.

Like Vicki, Marsha was a preemie, having been born after only a six month pregnancy, and, as a result, had developed a condition of retinopathy of prematurity (ROP). Unlike Vicki, however, she has always had some limited vision. In this respect, Marsha told us:

> I have some vision in my left eye, not a whole lot. I don't have any reading vision—I can't read print at all, but I can see, like, people and stuff, but they look ... blurry.

Further inquiry established that Marsha's actual vision was extremely poor (for instance, she uses a guide dog), so she was classified in the severely visually impaired category.

In regard to her NDE, Marsha, who was at home at the time, reported to us that she lost consciousness for more than a half hour during which time her fiancé later told her he could not detect a pulse. Marsha herself remembers a feeling of sinking into her bed, of falling "down, down, down." And, then, in her own words:

> And then things started to fade. There was no more pain, everything was different. [Now] instead of going down, I was going up. I was, like, in this tunnel. It was a long tunnel. Black.

I could see the tunnel. It was black. And I go into the tunnel. It was like I was being pushed. Like a vacuum cleaner or something. It was like a round narrow tunnel. Like only one person could pass in the tunnel. It was almost like wind in there. And once you go in the tunnel, you go forward, and you have to go up. There were lots of tunnels [with] other people. Each one in their own tunnel.

The more you go in the tunnel, the more peace [there] is. It's almost like wind, but it's peaceful. And as I get closer, I hear the bells ringing. I hear them more when I get closer. It's all this music and bells, not like bells here, it was different.

And you go and you see this light, like a little tiny white light far away. And then you get closer, and the light gets more bright. It gets brighter, bigger, and the closer you get, the more it fill[s] the whole tunnel.

And then you gotta go to the light, you want to go to the light, you don't want to go back. You want to go there. You go to the light—it's peace, no pain. It's like everything. It's like peace, voices, people and angels.

First, all I saw was the light and [then] I hear the voice. [And it says], "Come to the Light." I know I have to go. I know it was like God or something. It was like you see the face in the light, but you can't see it really—see the face, you know? But you see the light. And it's a different light. It's not like light on earth or sunlight. It's like white light but [more] like golden-white light. And it moves, it shimmers. It's not like any kind of light in the world. It's warm—like you were in the light. Not only [do] you see the light, but you become part of the light and the light goes around you. It's like God in the light. Nothing on earth is like that.

So I come, and there [were] angels. They were white and they had bodies, but it was not like our bodies. You could see through them almost. They say, "You come here, but you are not going to stay. You have to go back."

Before she returns, however, Marsha is shown something further.

They take me and show me big rooms with thousands or millions of people. They were sitting there and standing there. I could stand in front and see these people all the way back. There were people I knew. People I didn't know. People I know who had died. My grandmother [who had died in 1975] was there. My aunt was there; she had died in 1982. There were babies there that had died [and] babies yet to be born. I couldn't see them but I know they were there.

I know my friend, Hank, was there. He had died in 1982. He was much handicapped when he was here. He was blind, and he had amputated fingers and amputated legs, and stuff like that. And he was there in heaven, but it was like his body was right there.

I saw all these people and the way everything

was—the peace. Then they say, "Now you have to go back, it's time to go back." And then I remember before I went back, it was like I could see the earth. I could see stars—white things, like bluish-whitish things that go on and off. I guess those were stars. I don't know, I never see stars. I could see myself on earth, [too].

I could see myself, my body. It was in the same place I left it. It looked just like me. I looked the same. I just wasn't moving. I was dead.

Then I go back, backwards, the way you came. You go back through the tunnel, you hear the music, only it's going the opposite way. Going back, it seems much faster for some reason—it was very fast to come back. Then, all of a sudden, pop! And you were back in your body. I wake up, and that's it. I mean, I woke up and I was asking for the light, you know, "Where's the light?"

These three accounts are sufficient, we believe, to exemplify our assertion that the NDEs of blind or severely visually impaired persons tend to show all the same features that are typical for sighted persons. This is true despite the fact that those who have been blind from birth, like Vicki and Brad, but who clearly describe visual aspects of their NDEs, obviously have had no prior history with or even a concept of physical vision. To be sure, not all of the NDEs described by our blind respondents are as rich in their narrative line as those we have summarized here—some are certainly more partial, as with the NDEs of sighted persons—but there is no question that the great preponderance of these NDEs conform to the familiar pattern outlined by Moody (21).

To examine this point from a statistical perspective,

which will also help to provide something of an overview of our findings here, we simply list in Table 2 a number of the common features of NDEs and show how often they are mentioned in the interviews of the twenty-one respondents in our NDEr category.

Table 2

Frequency of Common NDE Features Mentioned in Interviews

Felt peace, well being,	20	(95%)
Reported a sense of separation from the physical body or an actual OBE	14	(67%)
Saw one's own physical body	10	(48%)
Went through tunnel or dark space	8	(38%)
Met others (spirits, angels, religious personages, etc.)	12	(57%)
Saw a radiant light	8	(38%)
Heard noise/music	7	(33%)
Had a life review	4	(19%)
Encountered a border or limit	6	(29%)
Was given choice or told to return to life	10	(48%)

In general, although the numbers in the various sight categories (i.e., blind from birth, adventitiously blind and severely visually impaired) were too small to permit any statistical tests, inspection reveals no obvious differences among sight sub-groups with respect to the frequency of NDE elements. Thus, whether one is blind from birth, loses one's sight in later life or suffers from severe visual impairment, the type of NDE reported appears to be much the same and is not structurally different from those described by sighted persons. Furthermore, with allowances for our small sample, the various features defining the prototypic NDE seem to be about as frequent as in samples of NDErs generally.

With these facts established, we can now turn our attention to our principal interest in this study, viz., whether and to what extent blind persons claim to be able to see during their NDEs and OBEs.

Chapter Four

Visual Aspects of NDEs
and OBEs in the Blind

To begin with, we will again consider the first three cases whose NDEs we described in the last chapter—Vicki, Brad, and Marsha—but this time, of course, with special reference to the visual aspects of their experiences. Following a review of these cases and a statistical summary of our overall findings, we will go on to discuss some further instances of apparent visual perception in other respondents, including some out-of-body experiencers (OBErs). In this chapter, we will also treat in some detail certain specific features of the NDE, such as the life review, which have particular relevance for the understanding of the mode of apparent visual perception in the blind. In general, as with the cases of Vicki and Brad, we will emphasize in this chapter the analyses of persons blind from birth since those instances provide the strongest and conventionally most inexplicable data pertaining to the proposition that the blind may actually see during their NDEs and OBEs.

Vicki

During a talk to an NDE support group in February, 1994, Vicki had occasion to declare at the outset in reference to both of her NDEs: "Those two experiences were the only time I could ever relate to seeing and to what light was, because I experienced it."

When asked by Greg Wilson what her very first reaction was to being able to see during her '63 NDE, Vicki replied:

> I was shocked. I was totally in awe. I mean, I can't even describe it because I thought, "So that's what it's like!" But then I thought, "Well, it's even better than what I could have imagined."

How well was Vicki able to cope with her initial experience of seeing? Not surprisingly, to begin with, it proved taxing because it was both foreign and disorienting to her.

As she said to Greg Wilson:

> I had a hard time relating to it [i.e., seeing]. I had a real difficult time relating to it because I've never experienced it. And it was something very foreign to me.... Let's see, how can I put it into words? It was like hearing words and not being able to understand them, but knowing that they were words. And before you'd never heard anything. But it was something new, something you'd not been able to previously attach any meaning to.

When we interviewed Vicki a few months later, she confirmed these reactions, but then went on to provide a sense of their unpleasant, even frightening, emotional tone:

> Vicki: It was very foreign to me to be able to perceive anything like that. It was very discomforting to tell you the truth. It was not a pleasant thing at first. It was

rather scary. I couldn't relate to it.

Interviewer: It sounds like it was disturbing to you.

Vicki: It was frightening.

Interviewer: Frightening? More than a distraction, then? Frightening?

Vicki: Yeah, because it was like I couldn't understand what was happening.

Yet, as disturbing as her initial experience of seeing was, at the same time Vicki, in common with some of our other respondents, claims that the fact of sight, in itself, was not terribly important to her. As she told us during the interview:

Interviewer: How important was seeing for you during this NDE as contrasted with other aspects of your experience?

Vicki: Not very.

Interviewer: It wasn't that big a deal?

Vicki: No. It was hard to adjust to, and in that sense it was a big deal. It was scary at first. Then, I liked it, and it was OK. I had trouble relating things to one another—what I was seeing and perceiving versus what I had touched and known the way I had known things all my life.... But a lot of people are surprised that it [seeing] had as little impact on me as it did.

Although a long commentary on the subject is not in order here, for anyone familiar with the work that has been done with previously blind persons whose sight could be surgically restored (e.g., Gregory, 1966; von Senden, 1960), Vicki's comments here will not be altogether surprising. Such patients often speak of the difficulties associated with "learning to see," and many have been tempted to find ways to decline the "gift" that medical intervention has bestowed upon them. Furthermore, Vicki's remark, "But it [seeing] was something new, something you'd not been able to previously attach any meaning to," echoes Annie Dillard's (1975) observation on von Senden's patients: "For the newly sighted, vision is pure sensation unencumbered by meaning (p. 17)." The similarities—and differences—between the immediate reactions to visual stimulation of our blind respondents and those of persons who as adults are suddenly confronted with a world of vision will be discussed again later in this book.

In any event, now that we have a sense both of the definiteness of Vicki's visual impressions and the difficulty she had initially in coping with them, let us turn more specifically to precisely *what* she claims to have seen. To preface our examination of her testimony, however, we need to draw a distinction between two types of apparent visual perceptions.

Obviously, Vicki's perceptions, like those of our blind respondents generally, fall into two distinct categories: first, impressions of the physical world from a subjective out-of-body vantage point and, second, reports of otherworldly environments. Just as clearly, only the former lend themselves in principle to external corroboration. Therefore, accounts of perceptions of "the things of this world" have a primary value from the standpoint of this research, which seeks to determine whether the claims of vision on the part of the blind can ever be shown to be veridical as well as conventionally inexplicable. Otherworldly visions, in contrast, though of considerable interest in their own right, are not evidential in this context. For these reasons, then, we begin with a closer look at what Vicki told us about her this-worldly out-of-body perceptions.

In this connection, it will serve us best if we simply quote from the interview we conducted with Vicki in May, 1994, supplemented by a follow-up interview a year later, concerning relevant aspects of her 1973 NDE.

Vicki: The first thing I was really aware of is that I was up on the ceiling, and I heard this doctor talking—it was a male doctor—and I looked down and I saw this body, and at first I wasn't sure that it was my own. But I recognized my hair.

Interviewer: What did it look like?

Vicki: It was very long ... down to my waist. Part of it had had to be shaved off, and I remember feeling upset about that.... And then I saw my wedding ring on my left hand, and I had my father's wedding ring on my right hand and a plain gold band that I had.

[She then overhears the doctor saying to the female present that it's a pity that because of an injury to Vicki's ear she could end up deaf as well as blind.]

Vicki: I knew, too, the feelings that they were having. From up there on the ceiling I could tell that they were very concerned, and I could see them working on this body.

[She tries to communicate to them, but she cannot and feels very frustrated.]

Interviewer: After you failed to communicate to them, what's the next thing you remember?

Vicki: I went up through the roof then. And that was astounding!

Interviewer: What was that like for you?

Vicki: Whew! It's like the roof didn't—it just melted.

Interviewer: Was there a sense of upward motion?

Vicki: Yes, mm-hmm.

Interviewer: Did you find yourself above the roof of the hospital?

Vicki: Yes.

Interviewer: What were you aware of when you reached that point?

Vicki: Lights, and the streets down below, and everything. I was very confused by that.

Interviewer: Could you see the roof of the hospital below you?

Vicki: Yes.

Interviewer: What could you see around you?

Vicki: I saw lights.

Interviewer: Lights of the city?

Vicki: Yes.

Interviewer: Were you able to see buildings?

Vicki: Yeah, I saw other buildings, but that was real quick, too.

Almost immediately after this rapid visual impression, Vicki is whisked into the tube and thrust toward the remainder of her otherworldly experience.

Unfortunately, both because of the lapse of more than twenty years since her '73 experience and Vicki's inability to identify the persons involved in her medical treatment, it is impossible to provide any external corroboration for her perceptions of the physical environment she claims to have had. Nevertheless, our pressing her on some of these points made it clear that insofar as Vicki herself is concerned, she is convinced that she actually saw what she reported.

At the same time, when she is less than certain about some of these details, she is quite frank in saying so. A good example both of her certitude and her qualifications is found in an interview concerning her perception of the rings she was wearing. In elaborating her answers here, Vicki went on to state:

Like I said, this is not absolutely clear, but I think

I was wearing the plain gold band on my right ring finger and my father's wedding ring next to it. But my wedding ring I definitely saw.... That was the one I noticed the most because it's unusual. It has orange blossoms on the corners of it.

We are left then with Vicki's testimony concerning her out-of-body vision as essentially an uncorroborated and inherently unverifiable self-report. Furthermore, it is of course possible to argue that she had means other than direct seeing to know that her hair was long and that she was wearing certain rings at the time. Nevertheless, it must also be noted that Vicki herself is not confused about the fact of her seeing, only about some of the details in what she has already admitted was an extremely brief, disorienting and sudden explosion of visual input. In addition, a further examination of other aspects of her experience, which we will now undertake, lends further weight to her assertion that she was indeed able to see during her NDE. Consider, for example, Vicki's experience during her life review.

Part way between the impressions of the physical world and those pertaining to a purely otherworldly environment stands the life review—a panoramic replay and reliving of seemingly virtually every event in one's life. In Vicki's case, she underwent a separate life review in each of her two NDEs, and in each instance, she again claims, as most sighted persons do, to have seen the events in her life, but for Vicki—at least during her '63 life review—this was of course the very first time that she had a visual representation of these scenes.

For most NDErs, the life review is the principal educative process of the NDE that allows the experiencer to have a comprehensive and almost omniscient understanding of his or her life through which the causes and consequences of one's behavior can be examined dispassionately and without judgment (apart from self-judgment). Because of the type of learning it instills, the emphasis in the life review is usually on feelings and emotions, as well as one's motives, and the purely visual aspects of the experience are secondary. This is especially true in Vicki's case since, as we already know, the visual component of her experience was not particularly important for her. Nevertheless, it is precisely that feature which is crucial for us, so we will stress what Vicki does not. This orientation certainly gives undue value to the visual side of Vicki's life review, at the expense of its pointed lessons for everyday life, but the latter must to some degree, at least in this article, be sacrificed in favor of what is more germane to our research interests here.

Let us begin here with Vicki's initial experience. As a child of twelve, she underwent a life review when she first emerged from the tube. And there is no question that she saw her life then, too, as she indicates in her interview with Greg Wilson:

Vicki: And then I saw my life—you know, my whole life so far—going in front of me.

Interviewer: You saw your life in front of you?

Vicki: Yes.

Interviewer: And you must have been surprised by that, because you were seeing.

Vicki: Yeah, I was. And it was like everything in a lot of detail, but yet it went by me real fast.

In our later interview with Vicki, we questioned her further about the nature of her life review in order to confirm and clarify some of the foregoing statements.

Interviewer: When that experience happened to you, was it more like you were seeing your life or were you, in a sense, reliving it?

Vicki: It was both.... It's like I could see it, feel it, taste it, everything. It was like it was all inside of me, but yet it was going past me.

Interviewer: It was a full sensory involvement in your life?

Vicki: Yes. It was like it was being played for me, too. It was like seeing a movie, but yet being in it at the same time—and yet I was separate from it.

Interviewer: When this was happening to you, could you actually see your life?

Vicki: Yes. I saw everything—and I also felt everything that I felt plus everything that everybody else felt.

Vicki then went on both in the interview with Greg Wilson and in ours to give a number of specific examples of various incidents in her life that she witnessed in her life review. We will present three of these episodes here.

The first one took place when Vicki was about eight years old while she was a student at the school for the blind in Oregon. It concerns another blind girl named Bunny who had a crucifix she cherished but which Vicki coveted for herself. As Vicki tells it:

> She lost it in the dining room, and I found it. And I heard her crying over it. I didn't tell her right away that I had it. And felt so guilty. And then I told her.... I said, "I just had to admit to you I borrowed it for a little while. And I didn't want to see you going through any more pain, so I wanted to give it back to you right away."

When this scene was played back for Vicki in her life review, she not only felt her feelings again and Bunny's but she saw where the event took place. In fact, she says that she "saw everything"—chairs, tables, beds, etc. "It was in the dormitory where I gave it back to her. And I saw our rooms. And I saw everything.... It was like it was in a movie."

When in our interview we asked Vicki to comment further on her perceptions at this time, she furnished an answer that gives us a great deal of insight into how her impressions in her life review were radically different from the way she was used to perceiving and interacting with her environment as a blind child:

> When I was going into the dining room or into the dormitory generally, of course, I would perceive the things by bumping into them, or by touching them, or whatever. This time I could see them from a distance. It was not like I had to be right on top of them, touching them, or sitting on them or whatever, before I was aware of them. I don't imagine things very well in my mind until I get there. I have a lot of trouble dealing with images of things when I'm not directly there. This time, it was like I didn't have to be right there to be aware of the chairs. I saw the metal chairs that we sat on as children and the round tables in the dining room, and they had plastic table cloths on them. I didn't have to touch the plastic table cloths to be aware of them.

In the same interview, we asked Vicki whether in her life review she ever saw scenes involving her two good friends, Debby and Diane, whom she encountered in both of her NDEs. When Vicki replied in the affirmative, we asked her to describe them to us.

> Diane was kind of crippled and having a lot of trouble with her movements. Debby was quite puffy and plump, and she had a lot of fluid retention problems. She had a shunt in her neck because she was hydrocephalic.

As it happened, Vicki shared the story of her experience with her housemother to whom she was very close and who believed her implicitly. And, interestingly for us, Vicki said the housemother was also able to validate her description of these two girls. "She said that that was indeed what Diane looked like, and that she was very delicate. Debby was indeed plumpish, and she did confirm that.... She did indicate that I was right."

Of course, since Vicki had previously hugged both of these girls and was aware of their condition, she had other sources of information on the basis of which to describe their appearance. But, once again, she herself is quite clear that in this instance, her impressions of them came from visual knowledge provided in the life review.

Vicki made a similar claim for our final example, which in this case involved a potentially violent scene with her grandmother who was mentally ill and who forced Vicki, even as a young child, to sleep with her and have frequent sexual relations. She described this incident originally to Greg Wilson:

> Vicki: There was a point when I was ten years old when my grandmother was lying on the couch and I wanted to put my hands around her throat because I hated her so much, because of what she was doing to me. And I can remember digging my fingernails into my palms, really, really hard.... And [then] I went into my room. And I

experienced that too.

Interviewer: But this time you could see...

Vicki: Yes, I saw myself doing all of it. And I saw my grandmother. And I saw myself.

Interviewer: So this was the first time you'd actually seen your grandmother.

Vicki: Yeah.

Interviewer: What was your reaction upon seeing your grandmother? Did you have reactions like, "Oh, that's what she looks like. Or, "I didn't think she would look that way"?

Vicki: No. I wasn't even really affected so much by how she looked as by the emotions that I felt at the time on seeing it.

In our follow-up interview, we nevertheless asked Vicki if she could give us a description of how her grandmother appeared in that incident. In fact she could, and this is what she told us she saw:

> She had short, curly hair, and it was of course gray. I knew that, but the color gray does not really mean a whole lot to me. But it was short and curly hair and she was kind of plump. She was shorter than I was.

Again, Vicki obviously had some conception of her grandmother's appearance before her NDE, but she did aver that this account of her grandmother's looks was based on what she saw during her life review, although she again emphasized that the visual representation of her grandmother was not of particular interest to her at the time.

These, then, are a few episodes from Vicki's life review as a child of twelve, and they are all consistent with her understanding that what she experienced then was shown to her in the form of visual images. The fact that these images were not nearly so important to her as what they were teaching her is certainly understandable—though they are of course of exceeding significance to us here, especially when they are coupled with suggestive indications that Vicki was indeed experiencing, however inexplicably, a mode of visual perception that until then had been completely outside her ken.

As we have already observed, Vicki had a second life review in '73, which was initiated by the phrase uttered by the luminous being she understands to be Jesus: "But first, watch this."

Immediately, she saw her entire life, beginning from her birth. This time, however, she spoke of her life review more generally and in terms of what it had disclosed to her:

> I saw my grandmother's abuse of me again. I saw my mother's abuse of me, and that she was wonderful when she was sober, but that she was not when she was drunk. I felt all those things again, and saw all of it again. I saw myself in school, the different ways that I'd felt. The selfish things that I had done. The loving things that I had done. How I affected other people when I did them. How other people affected me. All of it.

In this second review, as Vicki made clear in her interviews with both Greg Wilson and us, there was a more mature kind of reflection possible, since Vicki was now in her early twenties, and a great deal was implied about the importance of self-compassion and not judging others. All this, however, was tempered with a certain wry humor that occasionally emanated from the being of light who seemingly was regulating this experience for Vicki, while also commenting on it and instructing her.

One amusing instance of this concerns the use of colloquial speech which Vicki, in agreement with other NDErs, noted is not disdained by the being of light who seems to speak to us in the argot of our own day and culture. In this episode, Vicki, in a fit of jealousy, had ripped off the buttons and all the lace from a fancy dress of a classmate. As she later told Greg Wilson, she was gently reproved for this impulsive action by the being of light in a way that almost made her laugh—and certainly makes us do so.

Vicki: It was like, you know, I could feel from Jesus [his] understanding and compassion about how I felt that way, and why I did it. But, you know, it was sort of like he talked to me during that time. He says, "Yeah, that wasn't too cool."

Interviewer: Really?

Vicki: The thought that came into my mind ... that he was giving me was, "Yeah, that wasn't too cool."

Interviewer: You're not kidding me?

Vicki: No. That's exactly what he said.

Once Vicki entered into the otherworldly segment of her experience, she was conscious of a distinct change in the nature of her visual perception. Specifically, what had been difficult to adjust to and profoundly disorienting when she was apparently first receiving visual input from the physical world now becomes easier and seemingly more natural for her. As she told us when we inquired about this matter, her perception here was "direct" and "more clear." In fact, Vicki went on to say, it was to her mind "the way it's supposed to be." Visual representation in the otherworldly realm, then, is no longer effortful or problematic—it is just the way it is.

Immediately Vicki claims to have been aware of seeing trees, birds, grass and flowers all arrayed in a kind of preternatural splendor and suffused with an all-pervading light. But even here, her vision is not necessarily identical with what we would expect a sighted person to report. For example, Vicki claims that she could not discern the colors of the objects she saw. When asked to describe the color of a flower, all she can say is:

> It was different brightnesses. That's all I know how to describe it as. And different shades.... But I don't know. Because I don't know how to relate to color, but I know it was different shades of light.... [Flowers] were different brightnesses of light.

Nevertheless, the perception of objects and persons themselves seems to have been visually normal for Vicki. She reports seeing, for instance, the five deceased persons she knew in life—her friends, Debby and Diane, her caretakers, Mr. and Mrs. Zilk, and (in her second experience only), her grandmother—and "intuitively recognized them." This was the case despite the fact that, as Vicki maintained, these persons appeared different to her in this setting than they did in her life review. In this otherworldly realm no physical or mental handicaps were present. "They had nothing amiss with them now," Vicki commented. We have already seen that, according to Vicki, her housemother had been able to confirm the general physical descriptions of Debby and Diane that Vicki claims were derived from her vision of them during her '63 NDE.

Perhaps her most detailed description of a person in the otherworldly domain is of the being she recognizes as Jesus. In our interview with Vicki, we asked her a number of probing questions about exactly how he looked to her and how she could be certain of his identity, beginning with her initial encounter with him in her '63 experience.

Interviewer: You saw a man whom you identified as Jesus, and in your interview with Greg, you described him pretty specifically. Can you tell me what you remember being aware of when you saw Jesus? How he looked and so on?

Vicki: I was real close to him. He actually hugged me. He embraced me, and I was very close to him. And I felt his beard and his hair. They were very close to me. He actually enveloped me—that's the only word I can think of to describe it. He enveloped me with so much warmth and love and with his actual physical presence type of feeling.

Interviewer: What did you notice about his hair? You said that you felt his beard and you noticed his hair. How was his hair shaped, for example?

Vicki: His hair, it wasn't exactly straight but it wasn't curly either. It was kind of coarse.

Interviewer: Was it long or short?

Vicki: Long, it was past his shoulders.

Interviewer: Did you see his eyes?

Vicki: They were piercing eyes. It was like they permeated every part of me, but ... not in a mean way. It was like you couldn't lie about anything, and he just looked everywhere and he could see everything. Yet I wanted to reveal everything to him.

Interviewer: Was he wearing any kind of clothing?

Vicki: Yes. And his beard had very bright lights in it. I mean in it.

Interviewer: Like jewels or streams of light?

Vicki: It was like lights came out of it.

Interviewer: Sparkles or more coherent forms of light? Maybe that's hard for you to answer.

Vicki: It was just light coming out of the beard itself.

Interviewer: What about his clothing? What type of clothing did he have?

Vicki: He had nothing on his feet. I could see the five toes. There was nothing on his feet at all. He had this kind of robe-thing on that didn't come all the way down to his feet. It was below the knees but above the ankles.... It was open, so that you could see his bare chest in the front. Then it had this sash around the waist part, and that was the only thing that was holding it together. There were no other fasteners on it at all, but the sash had falling ends, almost as though it was living.

Interviewer: Vicki, this is not meant to be a skeptical question but I want to forewarn you that it might sound that way. Did the impression of Jesus that you had correspond to your expectations about him from what you were familiar with by reading the Bible and perhaps from other forms of your religious training?

Vicki: I don't really know because I couldn't picture it. I know that sounds really stupid possibly, but never having seen, I have no real image of it. I couldn't really comprehend what the Bible said about it anyway.

Interviewer: When you had this experience, even though it was a revelation to you from the standpoint of never having had a visual representation of Jesus before, did he identify himself to you as Jesus or did you just intuitively know that it was he?

Vicki: It was like I intuitively recognized him and knew that it was he. He also said to me, "You cannot go to my Father's house now."

Interviewer: How did he communicate that to you? Mentally? Telepathically?

Vicki: Words, it was words, but it was not vocal. It was like directly into my mind.

Interviewer: Was there a brightness associated with Jesus?

Vicki: Much more than anybody there. He was the brightest of anybody there at all.

Interviewer: Was it a hard brightness to look at? Was it unpleasant?

Vicki: No. It wasn't unpleasant, but it was incredibly beautiful and warm. It was very intense. I know I couldn't have stood it if I were myself ordinarily, but because I knew I was not myself ordinarily, I knew I could stand it.

When we asked Vicki whether the image of Jesus she encountered in her '73 experience was the same or different, she unhesitatingly replied, "the same."

The entirety of Vicki's testimony concerning what she was aware of during the otherworldly portions in both of her NDEs is consistent with the assumption that she had a clear, detailed and a natural-seeming visual representation of the persons and environment of that domain. The fact that she was unable to discriminate colors in that realm (and was also unable to do so in the physical world) only adds plausibility to her account, since, as she says, she had no previous basis on which to understand the meaning of color. At the same time, it is hard to evaluate her perception of the being she understands to be Jesus. On the one hand, Vicki, as a deeply religious person, even as a child, would certainly be familiar with descriptions of Jesus. On the other hand, she maintains that, because of her blindness since birth, these descriptions never had formed any coherent pictorial image in her mind of Jesus. If we take her avowal not only to be sincere but truthful, the fact that her portrait of him accords so well with tradition is surely a puzzle worth pondering. As it is, all we can do here is to conclude that regardless of the source of Vicki's image of

Jesus, her account of her interaction with him is still another reason to believe that what Vicki experienced in the otherworldly realm, she saw.

Brad

As with Vicki, it will be useful if we begin our consideration of the visual aspects of Brad's experience with a more detailed account of just what he claims to have been aware of during the interval when he first found himself floating above his physical body until the time he is sucked into the tunnel through which he is transported to the otherworldly realm. In what follows, we will be quoting some excerpts from our original interview with Brad on July 9, 1994.

Interviewer: When you started having trouble breathing and you felt yourself lifting out of the body or floating up, when you got above the bed and ceiling, did you see your body at that time?

Brad: When I got to the ceiling?

Interviewer: When you were still in the room.

Brad: When I was still in the room, when I came to the ceiling, I noted that my body was still on the bed.

Interviewer: You could in some way or some form see your body on the bed?

Brad: Yes.

Interviewer: Did you know it was you? How did you identify that it was you?

Brad: The body that was on the bed was absolutely still and did not have any movement. I felt that it was something that must have come out of me and drifted up to the ceiling. Something that was left of me would be still on the bed. For a very brief moment I wondered why I felt like

I was sort of two people at the same time. I saw one part of me absolutely still as if being ready to be detained, and yet there was a very integral, important part of me that was about to float up beyond the ceiling to this new realm wherever it might have been.

Interviewer: Is there any way you could describe what you looked like at that time in terms of your hair or what you were wearing or anything in the room?

Brad: Are you talking about while I was in this...

Interviewer: While you were in your room above your body; any time before leaving the room?

Brad: I think I really did not pay attention to what I looked like on the bed. I was so frightened of what was about to happen that I just noted my body's presence on the bed, but didn't really notice any details.

Interviewer: Was there anything or anyone else that you saw before leaving that room?

Brad: When I was around the ceiling area, I did see my roommate, and at this time he was awake and beginning to shift around in the bed. Afterward I found out that apparently he knew I had been gasping for air. He knew that something had happened, and he got someone's attention. When I saw him, I saw him waking, sitting up, and standing up, and he was attempting to go out into the hallway. He, himself, also being totally blind, was not going very quickly at the time. He had more mobility limitations than I did, but he was moving out into the hallway. I have since found out that he was trying to get help. But that was the only note that I made.

Interviewer: You then later confirmed he had in fact gotten up to call for help? Was there anything that you noticed about him? Or about the sheets, or the bed, or anything in the room?

Brad: Well, I did notice about me that my body seemed to be extremely rigid and actually seemed to be cooling as if it was losing some sort of essential warmth. It seemed to have no expression whatsoever. Also my roommate's sheets were piled partly on the floor and partly on the foot of the bed.

Once again, it's clear that despite the very rapid shift in awareness Brad reports at this stage of his NDE, he nevertheless was able to remember and describe significant features and movements within his physical environment at the time. Although it is of course impossible for us to provide independent evidence (for example, from testimony from his roommate at the time of this incident) that could support Brad's account, he, like Vicki, speaks with great assurance about his visual perceptions here. Moreover, and to an even greater extent than was true for Vicki, Brad's narrative of what he was aware of once he seemed to be hovering above the roof of the school is remarkable for its clarity of vision.

Interviewer: Now I would like to move on to where you said you were penetrating the ceiling through the third floor and to the roof. Do you remember if the building was three floors or four floors?

Brad: Three floors.

Interviewer: So after the third floor, you came to the roof. Did you see anything on your way up either through the third floor or when you got to the roof?

Brad: I didn't really take any note. It seemed that I was being propelled so quickly that I really did not have a chance to look around at any of the floors.

Interviewer: Okay. And when you got to the roof, did you see anything there like space or outdoors or anything like that?

Brad: I think that, for a moment when I got to the roof, I did notice the outdoors. I knew there were streets around where I was.

Interviewer: Knew or saw?

Brad: I clearly visualized them. I could suddenly notice them and see them.

Interviewer: And what did you actually see?

Brad: I remember a trolley going down. Boston has a large trolley system, and I remember there was a trolley passing very close on the same street as the building I was in. There were two playgrounds where the children in this particular center would play. I remember seeing what we could call the backyard which was on one side of the building, and I remember that I could see a hill that I used to scamper up and down just for exercise in the part of that yard that was farthest from that particular building. Those are the sights that I can particularly remember seeing. I wondered, even then, how I could know them without touching them. I could actually point to them.

Interviewer: Do you remember when this happened? Was it in the evening or the day?

Brad: It was in the very early morning. I would guesstimate around six-thirty or seven o'clock that morning. I vaguely remember when I woke up asking what time it was, and I was told it was about seven-thirty in the morning.

Interviewer: Do you remember seeing the sun or seeing light come up when you got to the roof and saw the street and trolley?

Brad: I believe it was cloudy that morning. We had had some snow the day before.

Interviewer: Did you see that snow?

Brad: Yes. In fact snow had covered that area at least a foot deep. It was a major storm. I remember that morning not seeing the sun. It was kind of cloudy and looking a bit on the muggy side. Very dark, generally a wintry kind of cloudiness, a layered kind of cloud, but I didn't spend much time looking at that because as soon as I had a look I was in that tunnel. The glance I did have was very quick. Didn't last long at all, maybe a few seconds.

Interviewer: But in those few seconds you were able to perceive the playing field and the snow on the ground. Do you remember the snow being positioned in any which way particularly or resting on any of the playground? Was there anything that struck your eye?

Brad: I think that everything except for the streets was covered with snow, thoroughly. It was a very soft snow. It had not been covered with sleet or freezing rain. It was the type of snow that could blow around anywhere. The streets themselves had been plowed and you could see the banks on both sides of the streets. I knew they were there. I could see them. The streets were slushy. The snow had fallen when it was almost at the freezing mark, so it was basically slushy. The snow was very soft, kind of wet. I don't remember anything in particular that the snow rested on, like trees or anything like that. I can't recall that.

What is perhaps most striking in Brad's narrative is the precision of his apparent visual perceptions during this stage of his experience, as, for example, in the description he has just given of the qualities of the snow that had fallen the day before. In this respect, the nuance and detail he reports are more impressive than Vicki's rather impressionistic account in the comparable phase of her NDE. What might account for Brad's extraordinary ability to etch these scenes so vividly for us in pictorial language?

It is certainly not his articulateness *per se* since Vicki, too, is very fluent and assured in her speech. And of course both of these persons were born blind and therefore lacked any experiential referent for physical vision. However, from our interviews, it is apparent that there was one highly significant difference between Brad and Vicki during their respective out-of-body experiences, and that is this: Whereas Vicki reports having been extremely disturbed at the onset of apparent vision to the point of being frightened by its distracting input, Brad himself, apart from some momentary confusion, seems to have taken it far more in stride. His recollections of his response in this respect were made evident to us in an interview we conducted with him on July 23, 1995.

Interviewer: If you could go back to that first segment again ... before you got into the tunnel. I know it was very fast, but during this time, would you say that you felt disoriented at all or not?

Brad: I was extremely aware before I went into the tunnel at all times. I was fully aware of it.

Interviewer: So you were not disoriented.

Brad: No.

Interviewer: Were you confused about what was happening?

Brad: Yes, only in the sense that I found myself wondering how I managed to get where I was, but those questions seemed to come so quickly that I really didn't have any time to ponder about them.

Interviewer: Right, because I know you were going so fast. Were you puzzled by what was happening? I mean, I guess it's slightly different from being confused.

Brad: I guess the best I can say is I was somewhat confused but not worried at all.

Interviewer: Yes. Again I want to focus just on the kind of data input side of it, just in terms of the things that you were aware of. Were you at any time frightened during the first part of this experience by anything?

Brad: Before I entered the tunnel?

Interviewer: Yes.

Brad: No.

At this point, since Brad, unlike Vicki, did not undergo a life review, let us follow him as he now enters into that tunnel and moves into the otherworldly portion of his NDE.

In connection with his passage through the tunnel, in our original interview with Brad we asked him if he had any awareness of color, something that Vicki had claimed she could understand only inferentially perhaps as "different brightnesses of light." Brad, whom you will recall was also born blind, likewise had a difficult time grasping this aspect of his otherworldly environment. In his own words:

> When I actually got into the tunnel, I do remember that one thing that puzzled me was the lack of any color. I began to wonder if this was darkness. By the time I got to the narrowest part of the tunnel there was no light going through. It was almost complete darkness. There was no color whatsoever. It was as black as I can understand blackness to be. But coming out into the large field, the closest I could tell you about color was that the brightness and brilliance of that whole area was absolutely indescribable. I could not distinguish fine shades of color, for some reason. It's possible that I could have, but I had no vocabulary to describe it. I've been told when I was a very young child of four or five that grass could be brown or green or that the sky could be blue, that water could have a blue color to it, or whatever. I knew that there were certain things that were certain colors, depending on the season and et cetera. But even then my concept of colors, my perception of colors, still remained

absolutely beyond my reach.

Unlike Vicki, however, Brad, as he indicates, was not able to detect subtle differences in brightness in the environment in which he now found himself. This is made clear in the following excerpt from the same interview:

Interviewer: When you saw the palm trees or the grasses...
Brad: Did I notice any differences in those?
Interviewer: Yes, exactly.
Brad: No. I didn't. It seemed as if everything was the very same bright, brilliant color, but there were no real differences that I could tell.
Interviewer: But it was clearly different than where you had come from in the tunnel?
Brad: It was almost diametrically opposite to where I had been.
Interviewer: Even though you couldn't distinguish differences in the brightness, it was all very brilliant?
Brad: Oh, extremely. It was so brilliant that it would shock me to even think about how brilliant it was. It was far more brilliant than anything anyone has ever described to me here on Earth.

But just as with Vicki, once Brad enters fully into the otherworldly realm, there is a distinct change in the *quality* of his visual perception. In his July, 1995, interview with us, for example, in commenting on this shift, he said specifically that compared to the first portion of his NDE, his otherworldly perception had "a heightened awareness." And in a follow-up interview, he was even more explicit on this point:

On its naturalness:

It was like it was always there.... It was so natural it was almost as if I should have always been able to see like that. It was as if I was saying to myself "hmmm, this is something beautiful." I couldn't understand why I never could do that back in my own body but yet it was so unbelievably natural.... I thought to myself I should be able to carry this right back with me. It's just something I've always had. You know, I felt that I've always had that kind of perception even though in reality I never had.... I was very comfortable with it.

On its clarity:

Things were extremely clear. I mean I could literally see everything around me for such a distance that I could not believe.... There were no shadows, everything was absolutely clear. And the light was everywhere.... During that experience, [everything] was so clear that there was no way I could mistake any one thing from any other. I could have pointed to anything within that realm and know that I not only saw it but could tell its dimensions ... [and] could be able to tell whatever peculiar markings or different peculiarities of that object, whatever it was. I would actually know it so clearly that it would almost be like I could see every atom of it, literally.

Once again, then, we see, as we did with Vicki, and as we will with still other blind respondents, that the otherworldly features of the NDE have a naturalness and immediacy in their visual aspect that make it seem almost as if what may be utterly foreign and incomprehensible to the world of the blind in their daily life is suddenly revealed to them as self-evident once they cross the threshold into the other world. In a word, sight there seems to be a given of one's experience and *does not have to be learned.* As Brad implied in his comments, it is something that he seemed always to have had, and to have known, and when it becomes manifest, it is recognized immediately and intuitively for what it is—a crystal clear vision that doesn't depend on the senses.

With regard to the *content* of Brad's otherworldly visions, as we have already seen, in contrast to Vicki, for whom the persons in her environment were the chief focus of interest, Brad was aware mainly of physical features and landscapes. Therefore, to give a representative instance of his visual experiences in the otherworldly domain, we will draw from his account of his approach toward the brilliant stone structure where the culmination of his NDE occurred.

> By this time, I was getting closer to the music and being absolutely fascinated by it. I wanted to join in with this music. It was absolutely precious. Within a very short amount of time, and I had no idea how much time had actually elapsed, but as I was going up the hill, I came to a large stone structure. I could tell that it was stone without even touching it. I could tell with some sort of sight that I had at that time, some sort of vision, I knew. They were almost like gem stones. They seemed to literally shine with their own particular light. Yet the light itself was actually penetrating right through the stones. It seemed that the stone was actually heightening that light, the light that was already there, to the point where I was almost afraid to touch those

stones. I thought that they might be fiery hot. In another sense, I was very curious about them. The structure I was going into was a large tubular structure. I would say that at first the tube seemed to be at least a hundred feet in diameter, with the top of the tube being well over a hundred feet above my head. Right up to the tube, there were palm trees and grass, and again this large field that actually existed all the way up to the entrance of this tube. When I got into the tubular structure itself, the ground suddenly changed, that is, the consistency of the ground under me. When I looked into the tube, I could tell that I was going to step on some kind of stone, the same shiny, brilliant stone that I could see all around the tube. It was smooth stone, very, very smooth.... As I entered the tube, the tube itself began to narrow, very much like the tunnel I had been in before, only this time the tube was not nearly as steep as the tunnel I had previously entered. I remember though that it didn't narrow nearly as much as the tunnel had. In fact, it only narrowed to about my height. By that time, I had gotten to the narrowest part of the tube, and I could start hearing plainly the music I had heard before. It was as if people were singing in several different languages.... As soon as I came to the narrowest part of the tube, however, there was a large firm arm. I would guesstimate that it was about the size of a very large man's arm, but I really did not have the chance to figure out the size of this arm. What I do remember is that this arm actually reached out from wherever it was in front of me, and it was as if this arm went across my chest. I looked around very quickly. I was startled by it, and I noticed there was a large man whose arm had reached out from just ahead of where I was in a wider part of the tube. I remember wondering what was about to happen. I felt as if my forward motion had stopped at that very point, at the narrowest part of the tube.

Our conclusion here is similar to that which we reached in Vicki's case. On the basis of Brad's testimony, which is impressive both in terms of its consistency and compellingness, there seems to be little doubt that he had a clear, detailed, and almost preternatural visual encounter with his environment during the otherworldly portion of his NDE. Again, if one did not know Brad was completely blind it would be almost impossible to tell from his transcript (apart from what he stated about his color perception) that this is a man who had no previous experience with the visual world. Instead, he describes it using the lexicon of a normally sighted person. His account, therefore, coupled with that of Vicki's, makes it very difficult to refrain from concluding that under conditions of an NDE, seeing is native to and self-evident in the blind.

Marsha

Marsha's case is mainly of interest here in showing how the visual perception of a severely visually impaired individual during an NDE is not only enhanced, but can become virtually perfect. In her interview with us, she made it plain that her heightened acuity pertained both to her out-of-body perception as well as to that which she experienced in the otherworldly portion of her experience. As to the former, Marsha told us that when she was coming back, she was aware of seeing her body. At that point, the interviewer asked:

Interviewer: Could you describe it? Could you see it in detail?

Marsha: Yeah, it just looked like me. I was, like, asleep.

Interviewer: And how was your vision, if I could put it that way, when you were looking down on yourself?

Marsha: It was fine.... It was normal.

Interviewer: When you say normal, you mean clear?

Marsha: Yeah, everything. There was no problem with it.

Concerning the quality of her otherworldly perception, she commented:

Interviewer: Were you able to see better than you could in the physical world?

Marsha: Oh, yeah.

Interviewer: What was your visual perception like in this room [where all the people were]?

Marsha: Everything, I could see everything.... All the people, all the way back. Everything.

Interviewer: In what way? Could you be a little more specific?

Marsha: It was perfect. It would not be like that here. There was no problem. It was, like, you know—everything, you could see everything. It was not like your eyes. I don't know what normal vision would feel like. It was not like your eyes see. It couldn't be my eyes because my eyes were back over here. I could see gold in the room. Gold on the walls. There [were] white birds and angels and all these people.

Interviewer: When you saw birds and the people

and the room, were you seeing it in detail or just like you see now?

Marsha: No, no. It was detail. It was white light. Everything was white light in there. And there was gold on the walls.

Later on, in elaborating on her perception of colors during this part of her experience, Marsha was similarly definite about what she was aware of:

Interviewer: And could you see it [color] clearly in the experience?

Marsha: Yes. Everything was the way it was supposed to be.

Finally, when the interviewer probed to get Marsha's further thoughts on her visual experience during her NDE, this exchange occurred:

Interviewer: If you had to say how much sight you actually had at the time of your experience, is there a way for you to describe it?

Marsha: It was, like, perfect. I don't see how it could not be perfect. I can't say I could see like I see now.... I could see everything [then].

Interviewer: Do you have any thoughts on the fact that you had vision during this experience?

Marsha: Well, see, it was vision, but I don't think it was my eyes. I don't know how it works because my eyes were back here, and since they are not right and I could see everything right, there had to be more special vision somehow.

Although Marsha still has some residual physical vision, it is clear that her comments echo both those of

Vicki and Brad concerning the quality of her visual perception, especially in the otherworldly realm. There, she sees perfectly and in detail that is astonishing to her and for which she has no explanation. And like Vicki and Brad, who had also noted the naturalness of their otherworldly vision, Marsha uses a phrase we have encountered before, specifically in reference to color perception, viz., "everything was the way it was supposed to be." (22) Likewise, her visual impression of her physical body seems clear and distinct, in contrast to her everyday vision. Overall, her testimony is as striking as it is consistent and shows that severely visually impaired persons, too, may find that coming close to death appears to restore their sight to normal, and perhaps even superior, acuity.

An overall statistical summary of seeing in the blind

As intriguing as the foregoing cases may be in regard to whether the blind have actual vision during NDEs, it will not have escaped the reader's attention that these instances nevertheless reflect the experiences of the same three respondents we presented earlier. As such, they comprise only 1/10th of our sample. The question naturally arises: How typical are these accounts of our entire collection of cases, including, of course, those of OBErs? How common is it, in fact, that the blind claim to see during these episodes?

To answer these and related questions, we need to take a moment now to summarize our findings as a whole in this respect.

Table 3

Reports of Vision in NDEs and OBEs

	Yes	Not Sure	No
NDErs	15	3	3
OBErs	9	1	0

First, let us look at Table 3 in order to get a quick view of exactly how many of our respondents report being able to see during their NDEs or OBEs. Of our 21 NDErs, 15 claim to have had some kind of sight, 3 were not sure whether they saw or not, and the remaining 3 did not appear to see at all. All but one of those who either denied or were unsure about being able to see came from those who were blind from birth, which means that only half of the NDErs in that category state unequivocally that they had distinct visual impressions during their experience. Nevertheless, it is not clear by any means whether those respondents, blind from birth, who claim not to have seen, were in fact *unable to see*, or whether they simply failed to recognize what seeing *was*. For instance, one man whom we classified as a non-visualizer told us that he could not explain how he had the perceptions he did because "I don't know what you mean by 'seeing.'" He was not the only person to admit such perplexity, so that, even among those cases we felt obliged to classify as not involving sight, the possibility isn't entirely foreclosed.

As a whole, however, our data here are quite consistent in indicating that the preponderance of our blind NDErs do indeed report vision during their near-death encounters, while only a minority are unsure about the matter or, in some cases, have no clear sense of sight.

How about the OBErs in our sample? If anything, evidence of vision is even stronger here. Nine of our 10 OBErs claimed sight. And if we include the five persons who had both an NDE and one or more OBEs on other occasions, the figures are still impressive: 13 out of 15. (In this connection, incidentally, one of the NDErs whom we classified as a non-visualizer from the standpoint of her NDE *did* report vision during her OBEs.)

Overall, the number of persons who indicated they had some kind of vision, either during an NDE or OBE, was 25, which is **80%** of our entire sample. Even for those blind from birth, the majority, 9 of 14, or 64%, likewise reported sight.

Given that some kind of vision is the rule for the blind, we can go on to ask, just *what* do they see?

Qualitative aspects of seeing in the blind

In general, blind people report the same kinds of visual impressions as sighted persons do in describing NDEs and OBEs. For example, ten of our twenty-one NDErs said they had some kind of vision of their physical body, and seven of our ten OBErs said likewise. Occasionally, there are other this-worldly perceptions as well, such as seeing a medical team at work on one's body or seeing various features of the room or surroundings where one's physical body was. Otherworldly perceptions abound also, and seem to take the form characteristic for transcendental NDEs of sighted persons—radiant light, otherworldly landscapes, angels or religious figures, deceased relatives, and so forth. Somewhat similar otherworldly perceptions are sometimes found for OBErs as well (we shall give some examples in a moment), though these, when they occur, are usually limited to seeing light, beautiful colors and meeting others. None of our OBErs recounted a life review.

How well do our respondents find they can see during these episodes? We have of course already noted that the visual perceptions of Vicki, Brad, and Marsha were extremely clear and detailed, especially when they found themselves in the otherworldly portions of their near-death journeys. While not all of our blind NDErs had clear, articulated visual impressions, nevertheless enough of them did, so that we can conclude that the prototypic NDE cases we presented at the outset are fairly typical in this regard.

For instance, one of our interviewees, who had been near-sighted, and whose sight perished completely as a result of a stroke at age twenty-two, told us in connection with seeing her body, her doctor, and the operating room during her NDE, "I know I could see and I was supposed to be blind.... And I know I could see everything.... It was very clear when I was out. I could see details and everything."

Another man who lost his vision in a car accident at the age of 19 had a comforting vision of his deceased grandmother across a valley during his NDE. In commenting on his clarity, he said: "Of course I had no sight because I had total destruction of my eyes in the accident, but [my vision] was very clear and distinct.... I had perfect vision in that experience."

Still another man, this one blind from birth, found himself in an enormous library during the transcendental phase of his NDE and saw "thousands and millions and billions of books, as far as you could see." Asked if he saw them visually he said, "Oh, yes!" Did he see them clearly? "No problem." Was he surprised at being able to see thus? "Not in the least. I said, 'hey, you can't see,' and I said, 'well, of course I can see. Look at those books. That's ample proof that I can see.' "

Finally, what about the nature of OBEs in the blind? We have already noted that visual impressions of some sort occur almost invariably in these episodes, but to this point we have not yet had an occasion to provide any examples of the overall texture of these experiences. Here we will offer just a few representative accounts with special attention again to their visual aspects.

One of our respondents, a thirty-seven-year-old woman, blind from birth, whom we'll call Cheryl, has had a number of OBEs. One of them represents the simple classic form of viewing one's body from an elevated position. One day while Cheryl was visiting her parents' house during the summer:

Cheryl: I was laying on my back. One minute on my back and the next minute, I feel, like, a tumbling sensation is the best way I can describe it.... And here I am, I guess you could say looking down.

Interviewer: From where, do you remember?

Cheryl: I was probably about ten or twelve feet in the air.

Interviewer: And this is the time you looked down and saw your body?

Cheryl: Yes.

Interviewer: And what could you describe about yourself? Do you remember anything?

Cheryl: I was dressed; I still had clothes on.

Interviewer: Do you remember how you were dressed?

Cheryl: Um, I had jeans and a t-shirt, no socks. I had a watch on my left arm.

Interviewer: And you were seeing all of this from the ceiling?

Cheryl: Yes, mm-hmm. I guess that's how you

would say it. How do you describe it? You know, you just know. And I don't know if you could say it was actually seeing, but you knew.

Interviewer: And again, did you know what your hair looked like, and what your facial features looked like?

Cheryl: I would say so, yeah. At the time, I had real long hair, and as far as facial features, you know, it happened so fast, one minute I was above my body, and the next minute, I was at my girlfriend's house.

This account is instructive for at least two reasons. First, it shows the evanescent, fleeting nature of these simple, this-worldly OBEs, which is typical of this phase of the experience for our sample. Second, Cheryl's narrative reflects the uncertainty which our respondents, especially those blind from birth, sometimes express concerning whether the language of vision is actually an appropriate modality to use to capture their sense of what they were aware of. We have noted this reservation already among our NDErs, and it is a point to which we shall have occasion to return several times in this book.

Another of our respondents, Helen, who is 45, and like Cheryl, blind from birth, described two of her OBEs to us. The first one occurred in a boarding house in 1974 when Helen was lying down. Asked if she saw herself on the bed, she said: "Yeah, I did. I wasn't too scared. I said, 'Oh, is that where I'm supposed to come back to?' Like somebody seeing a landmark." The interviewer then inquired whether she was surprised to see herself to which Helen replied, "Yeah ... but I wasn't very surprised. I said, 'Oh, well, that's who I am and I'm on this bed and I'll come back.'" Later in her experience, she reported seeing trees and plants and various people walking around outside. About this portion of her experience, she commented: "Ooh, I was excited. It was, like, wow! What is this?... And I thought,

"Oh, did I get my sight back?"

In 1985, while living in England, Helen had another OBE in which she saw herself from up above sitting in a chair. "Yes, I could see somehow back.... I was sitting there. I was happy. I wasn't scared or anything. And I didn't look like I had died, I just looked relaxed." As in her earlier OBE, she again found herself floating outside her room and claimed to recognize certain of her friends walking to various shops in the neighborhood. In this connection, Helen remarked that not all of them looked the way she thought they would.

In these experiences, Helen also mentioned that she encountered a light about which she said, "It was intense. It was kind of warm and it was friendly.... It was just very bright."

A third respondent, Joyce, who has had both NDEs and OBEs, told us that during her OBEs she was able to go beyond the physical world on several occasions and enter transcendental realms where she could see. She too, however, has been blind from birth. In what follows we will present just one segment of one of these experiences where she saw beautiful flowers.

Joyce: I went into this beautiful flower garden. The temperature was maybe 85 degrees and the birds were singing, and the colors—though I have never seen colors— were quite vibrant and striking.

Interviewer: Did you see the flowers as well?

Joyce: Oh, yeah. I saw them and I saw the colors. I called a friend and I said, "Are there purple and yellow flowers?" She said, "Yes, there are purple and yellow flowers." And I said, "And pink?" And she said, "And pink and red." So I can remember all these flowers.... The flowers were the most vivid thing.

Interviewer: Would you be able to describe the

shape or the size of the flowers?

Joyce: The only thing that I can really remember about the flowers is that they were, like, larger than normal, softer than normal. I don't know how I would know this, but more brilliant—the colors [more] magnified than they would be on Earth.

Again, we find ourselves faced with the apparent paradox that a woman who has never seen and could have no obvious way of distinguishing colors appears to do both during an OBE.

These, then, are some snippets from our interviews concerning OBEs, and, as will be clear, they are generally consistent with what our NDErs tell us concerning the visual aspect of their experiences.

In summary, as a whole, our interviews with both NDErs and OBErs offer abundant testimony that reports of visual perception among the blind are common, that their impressions concern both things of this world and otherworldly domains, and that they are often clear and detailed, even in narratives furnished by those who have been blind from birth.

With these general statements now establishing an overall context for the findings of our study, we can return to a more detailed consideration of some further cases of NDEs in order to provide more evidence of certain visual aspects of these experiences as well as to bring out some critical interpretative issues that have so far only been hinted at.

Debbie

Debbie is a forty-eight-year-old woman who, like many in our sample, was born premature, given too much oxygen in her incubator, and consequently lost her sight at birth. Although she suffers from ROP, she does have some limited light perception and thus can distinguish light from dark. She cannot see detail and has no distance vision whatever, but she can, for example, detect visually if someone is standing in front of her, even though she may not be certain it is a person.

Like Vicki, Debbie has had two separate NDEs. Here, we will concentrate on the first, which took place when she was 25. In this connection, however, we will only summarize her NDE as a whole in order to focus our attention on its visual components, which are many and striking.

Shortly after Easter Sunday, 1971, Debbie was at home recuperating from a serious burn injury for which she had previously been hospitalized for over two months. While brushing her teeth, she fell unconscious to the bathroom floor, feeling that she might be dying. She immediately found herself enveloped in and going through a light. "And all the while I saw this beautiful light and it was different colors; it was, gee, what can I say? Colors I couldn't even begin to describe. It was fantastic." Simultaneously, however, she was aware of her physical environment, and could see her body lying on the floor while her concerned mother bent over her.

A being presents himself, comforts her, and helps her to cross over a bridge. She sees other people, including her deceased grandmother, who introduces herself to Debbie, and who shows her some of her friends and ancestors. She soon encounters another presence whom she understands is God and begins to plead to be able to stay. Before acting on her plea, however, this being imparts a great deal of information to Debbie concerning future events, including the person she would marry and that she would have a beautiful baby girl (both of which have come true, Debbie said), and tells her that she will have to teach people when she returns to life. Debbie protests, saying, "No, no, please, *please,* I don't want to leave this, please." All the same, she is sent back and comes to for a moment to find herself being attended to by her mother and a neighbor. Later she learns that she has had a seizure.

To highlight the visual features of Debbie's NDE, we will now quote some extracts from our interview with her.

Interviewer: When you were going through this experience, did you see anything?

Debbie: Oh, wow, you know what, I saw, like in stereo, colors that were undescribable, colors that we don't have words for.

Interviewer: Had you ever seen colors before? How did you know they were colors?

Debbie: Oh, gosh, I just knew because of the brightness of the different lights, the difference. And it translated into colors and it just, I couldn't describe what they were. People asked me what color. I said, "gosh, I can't describe it." It was just beautiful and I saw in stereo.

Interviewer: What do you mean when you say you saw in stereo?

Debbie: Well, like two different things at once. Or, I'd see this: me lying on the floor, and then I'd see my [deceased] grandparents. [Then] I'd see my Ma bending over me, and my grandparents at the same time.

Interviewer: Was this the first time that you had visually seen your mother?

Debbie: Oh, yeah.

Interviewer: And you saw your body as well on the floor?

Debbie: Yeah.

Interviewer: Could you describe your mother?

Debbie: Oh, gee, my Ma had gray hair, she was short ... about just five feet.... And she was in her bathrobe. And I told her she was in her bathrobe, and she said, "That's right, I was."

Interviewer: Did you see the color of her bathrobe as well?

Debbie: I thought it was a dark color.... And I think she said, "Yeah, it was black."

Interviewer: Did you see yourself for the first time as well?

Debbie: I saw this thin girl, maybe brown hair ... with maybe a little bit of gray, you know, beginning ... and quite young. And no wrinkles or anything. And I knew it was me. I just couldn't believe it though, because I thought, wow, I was face down, sprawled.

Interviewer: Was this the first time that you recall having sight?

Debbie: Yeah.

Interviewer: Did that surprise you?

Debbie: Yeah, I didn't want to be back in this little body because I knew I wouldn't be able to see in it.

Interviewer: Was there a period you needed to adjust visually or was it immediate that you knew what was going on?

Debbie: It was immediate. I knew it was, I was my soul. I knew.

Interviewer: Was this the first time that you also saw your grandmother?

Debbie: Yeah.

Interviewer: Can you describe what she looked like?

Debbie: Oh, gee. See, I had never seen my grandma, either as a young woman or an old woman. But she had brown hair, and my Ma said, "Yeah, she had brown hair." And she was a young woman. And I would guess her to be no more than thirty. She was, I mean, nobody seemed old there [laughs], nobody.

Interviewer: Did you recognize anyone else?

Debbie: Oh, yeah. This girlfriend I had who died of nephritis, Darlene. I recognized her right away.

Interviewer: Without her saying who she was?

Debbie: Yeah, she said, "Hi Debbie." I said, "Oh, Darlene."

Interviewer: How did you recognize her?

Debbie: She said, "Hello, Debbie," and it was just like her voice.

Interviewer: Was it a voice like we're talking?

Debbie: Yeah.

Interviewer: Was this the first time you had seen her?

Debbie: You mean since she died, yeah.

Interviewer: Not since she died, but ever, because I'm assuming you saw what she looked like.

Debbie: Oh, yeah, yeah, this beautiful young girl. And, yeah, it was the first I'd ever seen her.

Interviewer: So you saw what she looked like?

Debbie: Yeah, and then she was thin. And when she was on Earth, she wasn't thin. She had a thyroid problem. She had nephritis, which would swell her up. She had a lot of other problems and kids made fun of her when she was little; they called her "little fatty" and stuff like that.

Later in the interview, after Debbie had a chance to describe her second NDE, she was asked to comment on the quality of her visual experiences during her NDEs compared to her normal (lack of) vision.

Interviewer: So these near-death experiences are, as far as you can tell or remember, the only times when you've actually had clear sight perception?

    Debbie: Yeah, it's weird.

    Interviewer: And you did recognize people?

    Debbie: Yeah.

    Interviewer: And clearly as would people with sight?

    Debbie. Oh, yeah. Maybe clearer.

    Interviewer: Your perceptions were clearer?

    Debbie: Yeah.

    Interviewer: All your senses or only that of sight?

    Debbie: No, everything.

Obviously, Debbie's case has many visual echoes of those we have presented earlier, particularly Vicki's. Like Vicki, for example, she is able to see and recognize her physical body; like her, she sees her deceased grandmother; like Vicki, Debbie also meets a being she takes to be God who imparts a great deal of information to her, instructs her as to her spiritual purpose on Earth, and tells her about a child she is to give birth to. While in the transcendent domain, Debbie also sees a deceased childhood friend, who seems to be whole and without the deformities she had when alive, and, like Vicki, Debbie experiences what she takes to be colors as the different brightnesses of the lights. Finally, as did Vicki, Debbie begs to be allowed to remain in this realm of bliss, but is sent back.

    Some of these features are of course common to many NDEs, but the particular patterning of all these coincident perceptions in two women who are both blind from birth seems almost eerily uncanny. In any case, it is precisely this redundancy of unusual visual and other information in the NDEs of the blind that makes this body of data as difficult to dismiss as it is to explain. At any rate, it is obvious that the overall structure of these NDEs, including their visual components, does not just rest on a single case or two.

Carla

Another respondent whose NDE has still other intriguing parallels to Vicki's is Carla, a forty-two-year-old woman who, though she, too, suffers from ROP, has some limited though highly restricted vision in one eye. It is only barely sufficient, however, for her to be aware of forms in their grossest aspect, so she falls into our severely visually impaired category.

Carla's NDE, which occurred in 1972 in connection with a hysterectomy, is of interest to us here primarily for two of its features. First, she had an unusually protracted and detailed visual impression of her body and the medical team while out of body during her operation. Second, she, too, reports having had a life review during which she *saw* herself as a child as well as other persons and events from her childhood. Accordingly, we will focus on just these two aspects of her NDE here, beginning with her out-of-body perceptions. In this context, the interviewer asked Carla:

Interviewer: Did you at any point see your body on that table?

Carla: Yeah, and I did look back, looking over my shoulder.

Interviewer: And you saw yourself?

Carla: Uh-huh. And I could hear them, I could hear them working on me, I could hear the sounds of the operating room.

Interviewer: And was there any distinguishing feature about you on the table? Is there anything that you could describe: the machinery, the equipment, where the doctors were?

Carla: The anesthesiologist was the one who was doing the principal work. And they were working the respirator.

Interviewer: You saw them working with that?

Carla: Uh-huh.

Interviewer: From what vantage point were you looking?

Carla: I was in the center of the room.

Interviewer: Above the scene?

Carla: Yes, yes, and the operating table was in the center of the room. And the telemetry was on the ceiling, you know, the screen for the telemetry was on the ceiling.

Interviewer: Did you see that while you were out of your body?

Carla: Yes, but I don't know how to read it, it was wavy lines. Sort of columnar, I guess.

Interviewer: What was?

Carla: The lines on the telemetry.

Interviewer: And anything else about the table or what anyone was doing or wearing?

Carla: Well, they wore greens. I know that for a fact.

Interviewer: But did you see it or do you just know it?

Carla: No, I saw that shade and later on I could equate it. I can't describe it. It's darker than white; it's not as bright as red; it's kind of medium. That's the only thing I could say.

Interviewer: So everyone was wearing greens?

Carla: Yes. My doctor was tall. Both of them were tall, but the anesthesiologist had white hair. He wasn't old enough to really have white hair but he had white hair.

Interviewer: Anything else that you remember? Was his hair covered or not covered?

Carla: It was covered, but, you know, from underneath. It was, like, a little line underneath—it didn't completely cover his head. And he had a lunarian type face—you know, a moon-shaped face. And he was quite concerned.

Interviewer: You mean the look on his face or what he was saying?

Carla: What he was saying, and his whole aura was quite concerned, you know. And the things he was saying, like, "This should not be happening. We're losing her. This should not be happening."

As Carla's NDE unfolded, she found herself in a brightly lit, very white room, where she became aware that her life was being discussed by a kind of spiritual guide: "The man described all the events of my life, good, bad, or indifferent: the loss of my children, my marriage, what I did before as a child, my childhood experiences." At this point, the interviewer asked her:

Interviewer: How did you feel as this person recounted the events of your life?

Carla: I could feel the feelings with each experience. It was like a telepathic exchange, you know. And I could hear little snippets of each experience very quickly.... You know, things I had said and feelings I had felt, and it was bizarre.

Interviewer: Did you see it from the perspective of you or as an observer?

Carla: No, myself.

Interviewer: When these incidents were scrolling back, what was your role in them?

Carla: Just myself looking at the events.

Interviewer: Did you see them visually or only auditorily?

Carla: Yes, both, visually and audibly.

Interviewer: Was it like the vision that you had before or was the vision different?

Carla: No, it was crystal clear.

Interviewer: Different from your physical vision?

Carla: Oh, yeah. It was like there was nothing wrong.

Interviewer: So you're saying it was crystal clear.

Carla: Oh, it was.

Interviewer: Were you able to see details of people that you had never been able to see?

Carla: Oh, yeah. But I saw, you know, myself [and] how I was dealing with people and the exact things that I had said, you know, to these people throughout each experience.

Interviewer: Is there anything ... that you can describe visually that you couldn't have seen before this? Did any particular event stand out?

Carla: Well, a lot of the events were from my childhood and events from school. And, yes, I could tell you that the plants on the school campus were really green ... the lawns were green, it was really pretty. I grew up tall and grew physically before my age ... and so the kids who were partially sighted used to call me "big barn." And I think that through this, as I could see myself on the playground or swimming or doing whatever it was I was doing, that I was not the way they depicted me ... that in actuality some of the kids who made fun of me were bigger and fatter than me, you know, and I could see this.

Interviewer: Did that surprise you?

Carla: Yeah, it really did. It gave me the feeling then that, "hey, you're not so bad." You know how when you have kind of an emotional realization. And so it doesn't sound like a big deal [but] it really was to me.... I thought that I looked like a really graceful person. Like "a lady."

Comparing Carla's experiences to Vicki's, we see that in Carla's case her OBE impressions were much more precise and focused whereas Vicki's were highly transient and subject to the emotional upheaval she felt at the astonishment of seeing in the first place. Perhaps because Carla had a history of seeing, however poorly, she could attend to the events taking place during her operation with less distraction than Vicki. Though, of course, it is also possible that in terms of actual clock-time exposure to the scene Carla had more of an opportunity to observe events than did Vicki, who, it will be remembered, almost immediately found herself drawn up rapidly toward and then through the ceilings of the hospital. It is also a matter worth noting that in addition to the detail described by Carla during her out-of-body episode, she claims to have been aware of colors.

Carla's life review, though not nearly so replete with specific instances as Vicki's, nevertheless seems to have had a similar form, both in terms of its emotional content and significance, and its visual aspect. Particularly striking here, of course, is Carla's assertion that, in contrast to her usual vision, her sight during her life review was "crystal clear." Here again, as with Marsha, another severely visually impaired woman we mentioned earlier, we see how the acuity of one's vision during an NDE can be enormously enhanced. In this respect, too, Carla's observations here are consistent with other testimony we have previously cited from our blind respondents in all categories that their sight during their NDEs or OBEs is often seemingly flawless.

In most of the accounts we have examined to this point, the respondent seems to be clear beyond doubt that he or she has actually *seen* what is being described, whether it is one's physical body or other persons (from up above) during a medical procedure, scenes from one's life during a life review, or the events and encounters that take place in the otherworldly realms of NDEs and OBEs. And, in fact, there is no question that quite a few of our respondents do indeed make these claims in just this way. At the same time, in the course of this study it also became apparent that, especially when pressed, some of our respondents would sometimes qualify their statements in such a way as to suggest that perhaps matters weren't quite so straightforward in this respect as might first have seemed to be the case. And, of course, we have already acknowledged that some of our respondents allowed that they were really not sure whether what they were experiencing was vision as we commonly think of it, especially those who have been blind from birth and therefore lack any meaningful concept of vision.

We have thus far, however, only hinted at some of these complexities in passing and will in fact need to defer a full consideration of this matter until our discussion chapter. But both to lay the groundwork for that discussion as well as to provide at least one instance of such a case here, we would like to introduce still another respondent whose observations concerning these ambiguities will prove most instructive and thought-provoking.

Marilyn

Marilyn is a fifty-nine-year-old adventitiously blind woman who was born with cataracts but at nineteen, as a result of glaucoma, gradually began to lose her sight completely. Not long afterward, she underwent an operation, but it was unsuccessful, and she has been totally blind ever since. When she was fifty-seven, she had a heart attack, which was the occasion of her NDE.

What makes Marilyn's interview of particular value to us in this context, however, is the way she speaks about whether she saw during this experience. At first, it seems quite clear that she did not. Afterward, it emerges that she did have sight—of a kind. Finally, she settles for calling her experience "semi-visual." As a whole, her interview shows the subtleties involved in such descriptions and the ease with which a researcher (or even a reader) could leap to an unwarranted conclusion on the basis of an incomplete but apparently definitive declaration. In short, interviews like Marilyn's should give us pause about our ready inferences concerning what apparent sight is actually like in the blind or even if it can fairly be called "sight" at all. On this question, we must at least for now hold off any firm conclusions, but Marilyn's comments will help us frame our questions with more precision when the time comes.

We begin with some of her initial statements in our first interview concerning her apparent failure to see when she was close to death. She is lying on the operating table of a hospital:

> The next thing I remember is that I was conscious of being on a surface which I thought was an operating table. And I understood that there were people lined up—I didn't of course see them; this was not a visual picture—but I understood there were people lined up within an operating room.... And then the next thing that I remember was that my consciousness or psyche, or whatever it was, was above where I had been lying. It looked—the picture, which was *not* visual, was sort of as I would have it, being totally blind—and it was a picture of my body on a bed and that my body was black, and it was blacker. I mean either, I guess, shades of blackness but it was blacker than

it had been at first and this indicated to me that I was dying.

Shortly afterward, in the interview, Marilyn was asked to clarify her statement:

Interviewer: Did you ever see or have any visual perceptions during this experience when you sensed that your body was on the table?
Marilyn: No, I did not.
Interviewer: Did you have a sense of what was happening to your body?
Marilyn: I had it somewhat the way I would ... have it now—like I'm in the room and would have it as I would have it now. But without actual vision. It was like a picture without vision.

In other words, Marilyn appears to be saying that she had formed a kind of pictorial representation of herself but did not actually *see* her body as though from an external vantage point, as a number of our previous respondents had claimed to do.

Fortunately, we had occasion to interview her about a month later because of Marilyn's desire to share with us some notes she had made about her experience in her diary in March, 1994, just after her heart attack. These notes read in part:

I remember a view of my body from above it, looking down toward my feet. I did not view my head. My body was extremely black. It lay on a lighter surface, which was next to the wall, which I took to be a bed. From that vantage point, the wall was on my left.

Now, because it seems as if her original diary entries implied that she might have had some kind of vision after all, Marilyn was again asked to speak to this matter:

Interviewer: You said you viewed your body from above and you didn't see your face. Could you describe again what perceptions you had? Were they of a visual nature? How did you actually perceive what you were aware of?

Marilyn: Yeah. It was as if the part—say you took a camera and you put it high up above a bed and you took the view from below the face, and you took the view of the bed and the body lying on the wall. It's like that.

Interviewer: Did you see that?

Marilyn: Well ... I can remember the outline. I can remember it didn't have—well, it had some of what you might describe as color because the body was black all over and it got blacker. I mean, if there are intensities of black, it did that.... But it had the outline of my body. (23)

Interviewer: And you could detect that in a sort of picture-like way?

Marilyn: Yeah, it was like I was there, looking down at it.

Now, this is quite confusing and apparently discrepant from her earlier account, since Marilyn seems to be affirming here that, like our other respondents, she did, after all, have some kind of a visual glimpse of her body from up above. And a few minutes later, she actually denies that all "this was in her mind" by declaring with some emphasis:

Marilyn: This is sort of like being there! This was sort of like I was looking down on it. I was focused, it seemed like I was next to that wall, high up. I can't describe exactly how high ... but high enough so I had a view looking down, as though my being were like a camera focused downwards, and I'm taking a picture. But it was like being there, not like in front of me forming a mental picture.

Interviewer: It was as if you were looking at the picture rather than trying to mentally create it in your mind?

Marilyn: Yeah, I wasn't trying mentally to create it. It was more like being there.

So here, in contradistinction to what Marilyn seemed to be implying earlier—that she had no visual perception during her experience—she now states that it was as if she were actually there, looking down at herself, as though she were taking a picture with a camera from that angle. Not surprisingly, the interviewer was a little baffled at this point by this reversal in testimony, so an attempt is made to get Marilyn to rectify these two quite different versions:

Interviewer: In our earlier conversation you said that you didn't have any visual perception throughout the experience. But from your notes and from what you are saying now it seems like you had visual perception, though you are not sure how accurate it may have been.

Marilyn: Well, I believe it was accurate—the details, like the bed, the wall, and the fact that I was on the bed were true. I believe the fact that my body was black was not necessarily true, but was meant to convey the process of dying. So it was a combination of knowledge, plus it was true.... It's very hard to describe—maybe the best way I can describe it is to say that it was a semi-visual impression.

In further comments, Marilyn makes it clear that although her form perception was clear in her out-of-body state, she doesn't think she simply saw what was below her in the same way that a sighted person, perched at that angle, would have been able to see. Her attention was much more focused on particular details, and even then some of what she reports being aware of, such as the apparent color of her body, had mainly a symbolic, not a literal, significance for her. Thus, her "semi-visual" impression was seemingly a bit of a composite based on some of the actual physical features of the situation *plus* their psychological meaning. Whatever it was, however, certainly does not appear to be any simple analog of what sighted persons would understand as physically-mediated vision.

Marilyn's reflections on the nature of her NDE vision should at least give us further reason to explore the nuances, linguistic as well as conceptual, of our narratives more sedulously before formulating our conclusions as to whether or in what sense the blind may actually be said to *see* during these episodes. At the same time, however, it would be very premature and, in our view, incorrect to infer that these accounts may in the end turn out to be nothing more than elaborate hallucinations or retrospective psychological reconstructions. That they are in fact authentic visions, however conventionally inexplicable, is not only suggested by their undeniable similarity to reports given by sighted persons and the compelling sincerity and wealth of convincing detail provided by our respondents, but by the evidence that points to their external corroboration by others. And it is precisely to this kind of documentation that we must now turn in our efforts to determine the ontological status of these experiences of the blind.

Chapter Five

Corroborative Evidence
for OBE and NDE Visions

Obviously, in order to demonstrate that the perceptions described by our blind experiencers are something other than mere fantasies or even complex hallucinations, it will be necessary to provide some kind of confirming evidence for them, preferably from other independent witnesses or from reliable documentation. But just here, not surprisingly, is where it proves difficult to gather the type of indispensable corroboration that would help to cinch the argument that what they report seeing is indeed authentic. The reasons, of course, will be apparent: In many cases (and here Vicki's and Brad's can stand as prototypes), the reported NDEs or OBEs took place so long ago that it is no longer possible to know precisely who the witnesses were or, even if their names were known, where to locate them. In other instances, potential informants have died or were not accessible to us for interviews. As a result, much of the testimony of our respondents is dependent on their own truthfulness and the reliability of their memories. As a rule, we did not have cause to question the sincerity of our respondents, but sincerity is not evidence and one's own word is hardly the *last* word when it comes to evaluating the validity of these accounts.

Nevertheless, in at least some cases, we are able to offer some evidence, and in one case some very strong evidence, that these claims are in fact rooted in a direct and accurate, if baffling, perception of the situation. In this chapter, we will therefore present some representative examples of this kind, beginning with instances of OBE-based perception and then moving on to a couple of NDEs. These accounts will begin with the weakest form of corroboration, that based on the respondent's own say-so, then to episodes that purportedly involve other witnesses, and finally to cases where there is a variety of external evidence based both on the independent testimony of other witnesses and external documentation.

OBE cases

A simple, but representative, instance of a claimed OBE confirmation comes from a respondent named Pat, a thirty-seven-year-old woman afflicted with ROP who has been blind from birth. When she was sixteen, Pat had a spontaneous OBE while sleeping over at a friend's house. As she tells it:

> I suddenly became aware of a floating sensation, like I was floating upwards. But it just felt like the senses [were] intact. I mean it just felt like I guess I would feel if I were awake, floating upwards. And I went up to the ceiling, and I was sort of in a horizontal position and sort of gliding along the ceiling. So I touched the ceiling and noticed the different textures, the different crevices that were in the ceiling tiles, and that sort of thing. And it was something that I had never touched before.... I guess I had never really thought about it, but I didn't know what ceilings felt like.... And the next thing I knew I was back.... I was awake, but I knew it hadn't been a

dream, it was just totally different. It was just, I just knew it hadn't been, I just knew it couldn't be, and I knew I would have to check it the next morning and verify it.

And so the next morning, I told my friend, "You know, you're going to think I'm crazy, but I've got to check out your ceiling!" ... So, I put something on the bed and climbed up on it and touched the ceiling. And I'm telling you, you can't believe the feeling I got when I reached my hands up there and touched it, and it was like, "That's where I was!" It was just exactly, the textures were just the same, the ridges in the ceiling tiles, there was just no mistaking it.... I've got it, like I say, it's one of those experiences that's burned into my memory now.

Unfortunately, the friend who might be in a position at least to confirm Pat's report of this incident died about ten years ago, so we are left only with this respondent's own avowal that this really happened to her in the way she recounted it to us. As such, it is an intriguing story of apparent confirmation, but it obviously lacks evidentiality. We should also note that, strictly speaking, even taken at face value it would obviously have to be regarded as a tactile rather than visual OBE.

Another variety of OBE, which we heard from several of our respondents, offers a slightly stronger degree of suggestiveness. This is the type of experience in which an individual finds himself or herself in a different location and is able to witness events in that environment. Afterward, it develops that there is independent evidence that what the respondent observed there did indeed take place. Carla is one such person who described an incident like this to us. Here is her story:

In 1983, while Carla was in California, her step-father lay dying in a hospital. One afternoon, at exactly 4:15p.m., Carla, who was tired from housecleaning and other chores, went to lie down and found herself projected during an OBE into her step-father's room at the hospital. "I was aware of being in his room and his nurse saying, 'He's going to go.' And he said to me, 'I give up.'" Immediately afterward, Carla became aware of two male spirit entities in the room who seemed to be there to escort her step-father into the first stages of his death journey, and she actually felt that she was able, as it were, to go part way with him herself and saw a great number of spirit forms waiting to receive and welcome her step-father into this realm.

That same evening, a spiritually-oriented friend of hers named Alan called her and said, "What happened to you at 4:15?" As Carla recalls: "And we described the same experience. He was at his work place and I was ... in my bedroom. And he described the same thing." What follows is from our interview with Carla.

Interviewer: He saw your father?
Carla: Yes, he was there, too.
Interviewer: Did he see you in that experience?
Carla: Oh, yes, we were together.
Interviewer: You saw him as well?
Carla: I did indeed.
Interviewer: And you saw the same thing?
Carla: Yes.
Interviewer: And you were able to report it?
Carla: Exactly.
Interviewer: The same people, the two men?
Carla: Yes.

Interviewer: And was the nurse helping him in the physical realm?

Carla: Yes, she was.

Interviewer: And you saw her in that experience, too?

Carla: Yes, I did .... Her tag said "Debbi."

Interviewer: You saw her tag?

Carla: Yes ... on the left side of her top and it said, "Debbi."

Interviewer: Did you know her name was Debbi?

Carla: I knew that he had a lot of nurses, but, no, I did not know. And I did call the hospital and I asked to speak with the nurse. I said I was aware that he was gone. And she said her name was Debbi.

Interviewer: Do you remember how she spelled that?

Carla: D-E-B-B-I. It was really unique.

Interviewer: Did Alan also see that?

Carla: Yes, he did.

Interviewer: Had you ever seen the nurse before?

Carla: No.

Interviewer: Was there anything else that stuck out that you remember about her?

Carla: Shoulder-length hair but it was back in, like, a braid. And an oval face, a fair face. And medium build.

Interviewer: Do you remember what color her outfit was?

Carla: She wore white.

Interviewer: Was it a dress or pants?

Carla: No, a pants suit, sort of like a polyester-type double-knit, only a little bit on the high end of polyester double-knit...

Interviewer: Did you ask her anything about the experience when your step-father went?

Carla: She said it was very quick, you know.... It was just like he just gave up.

Interviewer: Did he actually say the words, "I give up," out loud?

Carla: Yes.

Interviewer: Did you ask her if he said anything at the end?

Carla: Yes, and she said he said, "I give up."

Interviewer: You asked her, "Did he say that?" Or did you ask her what he said?

Carla: I asked her, "What did my Dad say?" I didn't want, you know, I didn't want to give her any leading thing. And she said that when he went, it was like a mist around him and she felt very calm.

Interviewer: Just to repeat that: The nurse said to you, "He said, 'I give up,'"

Carla: "I give up."

Interviewer: And then he passed?

Carla: Uh-huh.

Interviewer: Apart from the whole event, did you ask your friend, Alan, too, what he heard your father say at the end?

Carla: I didn't have to. He told me.

Interviewer: So he said he heard that as well.

Carla: Yes, he did.

Interviewer: So the three of you independently witnessed the event.

Carla: Uh-huh.

We were unable to interview Alan or Debbi to get their version of this episode, so, once again, we are reliant on Carla's own testimony. If it is reliable and truthful, it is quite a tale of the apparent accuracy of OBE visual and auditory perception at a distance in a severely visually impaired individual. As it is, we can only let the story stand on its own and draw no definite conclusions about it.

Another similar episode, however, does have a measure of independent corroboration since in this case, the person observed in an OBE state was in fact another of our respondents in this study. Thus, in this instance, we can compare the report of the OBEr herself with that of the person the OBEr claims to have seen. This incident involves the woman, Pat, whom we introduced at the beginning of this section, and her friend, Cheryl, whom we mentioned earlier in connection with OBEs in the blind. We begin with Cheryl's account.

One night, when Pat was visiting a mutual friend, Irene, Cheryl had an OBE and found herself at Irene's house where she noticed Pat throwing up in the bathroom.

> And she was in front of the toilet, on her knees, and her left hand was holding her hair. She was sick and when I woke up the next morning, I felt terrible. I physically felt awful, which is really weird.... And I called Pat that day, and I asked her, "Were you sick at Irene's last night?" And I think she was hung over, too.... And I remember telling her, you know, I described what she looked like as far as her hand holding her hair, her left hand, and she was really embarrassed, to say the least.

Cheryl went on to give a detailed description of the fixtures of the bathroom, and precisely where she felt herself to be in relation to Pat when she was observing her:

Cheryl: ... the bathtub was sitting to the right of the toilet. And there was a hamper. It was in front of the bathtub, like in a corner. And the toilet paper was sitting to the right of the toilet. There's, like, a little, you know, like a little square divider thing. And there was a towel hanging on the towel rack right next to the sink.... I was facing Pat ... so the bathtub would have been to her right. The sink would have been on her left.

Interviewer: You were looking at her back?

Cheryl: Yeah, I think that's how I knew it was her left hand. I have no idea how I knew it was her left hand. But it was her left hand that was holding her hair back.

Interviewer: And do you know where in the room you were?

Cheryl: I was standing in the doorway. So ... I needed to have turned left, to have faced, you know, her back. So I was just in the doorway.

Now, here is Pat's version of this event (24):

We, Irene and I, were, you know, having a party.... Anyway, we had a few too many to drink and I ended up getting sick. And Cheryl called and said, "Irene, did somebody get sick at your house last night?" [And] Irene said, "Pat was sick," and Cheryl said, "Well, put her on the phone." And Cheryl went on to say to me, "I tried astral projection last night and I came to Irene's house.... Oh, it was the worst experience I ever had.... I knew I was at Irene's house, and all of a sudden I knew I was in the bathroom...." And you know, Cheryl was in the bathroom when I had gotten sick and when it happened she felt like she was tumbling over and over and over.... But she told me, she mentioned the motions that I went through. I've got real long hair, and she said she

knew that I took my left hand and I was holding
onto my hair and everything like that.

In this case, we can see that these two stories jibe
quite well in their particulars and, unless it is entirely
fraudulent, it seems to be a good instance of apparent
paranormal perception during an OBE with external
corroboration of its occurrence. However, since Pat and
Cheryl are friends, and this episode happened years ago,
their accounts are not truly independent and may be subject
to retrospective assimilation. Still, it remains a suggestive
story—one of quite a few in our sample—that the blind can
indeed register events in an accurate fashion while in an
out-of-body state.

Our last example of apparently veridical OBE
perception in the blind involves a man who saw himself.
What makes this case of special interest, however, is that he
also saw something he couldn't have known about by
normal means. Furthermore, he claimed that a friend of his
was in a position to confirm his report to us. Let us, then,
examine this episode, as told to us by a man we'll call
Frank.

Frank is sixty-six, but lost his sight completely in
1982. He cannot see anything now, including light or
shadows. He has had several OBEs, however, since
becoming totally blind. What follows is his recall of one of
them.

Around 1992, a friend of Frank's was going to be
driving him to the wake of a mutual friend. As Frank
remembered the incident:

> And so I said to her that morning, I said, "Gee, I
> haven't got a good tie to wear. Why don't you
> pick me up one?" She said, "Yeah, I'll pick you
> up one when I get down to Mel's [a clothing

store]. So she picked it up and dropped it off and said, "I can't stay. I've got to get home and get ready to pick you up to go to the wake." So I got dressed and put the tie on. She didn't tell me the color of the tie or anything else. I was laying down on the couch and I could see myself coming out of my body. And I could see my tie. The tie that was on. And it had a circle on it, it was red, and it had a gray circle, two gray circles on it. And I remember that.

The interviewer then probes for further details and clarification:

Interviewer: Now just for the chronology of it, you were lying down with this tie on, you saw yourself going out of the body, and then you saw the tie?

Frank: I saw the tie 'cause I told her the color.

Interviewer: You told your friend who was driving you?

Frank: Yeah, when she came back to pick me up.... And when she came down to pick me up, I said to her, "Are the circles gray in this tie?" And she says, "Yes."

Interviewer: Was she surprised that you knew?

Frank: Yes. She said, "How did you know?" She said, "Did anyone come here?" I said, "No, nobody came here." You know, you can't tell 'em [laughs], 'cause they just don't accept; they don't believe in it.

Interviewer: And do you remember what the tie looked like even now?

Frank: Yeah. It's a rose-colored tie with circles on it and dots in the middle of the circle. Whitish/grayish circle around there. And it's a beautiful tie, 'cause every place I go they remark on it. So she said to me, "Who told you?" And I said, "Nobody." I said, "I just guessed." I didn't want to tell because, like I said before, you can't say things to certain people.

Naturally, after hearing this story, we were eager to see if we could track down the woman involved in this incident. That proved difficult, since Frank had lost contact with her, but eventually he was able to locate her and, without telling her exactly why we were interested to talk with her, put us in touch with her. One of us (S.C.) conducted an open-ended interview with this woman shortly afterward and summarized it as follows in her notes:

> I independently called his friend who said she did purchase a tie for Frank that day and did pick him up for the wake. However, she didn't have a clear recollection of the sequence of events that day to confirm the accuracy of Frank's story and didn't remember the exact design and colors of the tie. She added that Frank is a down-to-earth guy who in her experience does not embellish stories. And even though she couldn't independently corroborate his account, she tended to think he was probably accurate in recounting the details.

So here, although we lack the crucial confirming facts we need from the witness involved, we nevertheless have a highly suggestive instance that this man's recall of his experience is essentially accurate. If it is, when added to the other examples we have supplied in this section, it is further evidence that OBE-based visual perceptions in the blind can, *at least at times,* be both veridical and seemingly impossible to explain in prosaic terms.

NDE cases

Here we will cite only two cases of apparently veridical visual perception in NDErs. Both of them have some degree of external corroboration to support these claims. Only one of them comes from our study, however. The other, and the first we will present here, was kindly furnished to us by a Swedish colleague, Ingegerd Bergström, a nurse and NDE researcher, after learning about our work at a lecture in Stockholm in June, 1994.

On that occasion she first told us about one of the subjects in her own research project on NDEs. The person in question, a woman whom Bergström characterized as "half-blind," was one of 34 patients Bergström and a colleague interviewed in their investigation. Of course, we were keenly interested in what her "half-blind" patient reported, and later on solicited a written account of this case from Bergström. Here is her description of it from a letter dated November 3, 1994:

> This woman had the ability only to distinguish light and darkness. She could, for example, see daylight coming through a window in an otherwise darkened room. She could not, however, make out silhouettes nor walk in dimly lit corridors.
>
> She had suffered from this limited vision for many years when she had a cardiac arrest at home. At that moment, she was sitting in the kitchen by her kitchen table. A sink was nearby, but she later claimed that she had not seen it for the past ten years.
>
> When this woman came to be interviewed, she arrived in a wheelchair, accompanied by her

husband, and agreed to allow the interview to be tape-recorded.

At one point, in asking her a question, I expressed myself badly by saying, "Did you on any occasion see...?" That was very embarrassing because I knew she was blind. Her husband reacted with disappointment, which was obvious to me by the look on his face and his body language.

But the woman herself, on the contrary, was pleased at the question, and answered: "It's fine you ask about that because there is one thing that I thought a lot about. When I had my cardiac arrest, I suddenly saw the sink with the surroundings—and I hadn't seen any of that for ten years."

The husband reacted with surprise, and wondered why she didn't tell him that. He always thought she told him everything. She answered then: "You never asked if I saw anything at the time my heart stopped." She then told how the sink "appeared out of the fog," and that there was unwashed china piled up in it.

That was the husband's responsibility and he looked very guilty, but at the same time angry, because she previously didn't tell him this.

This case is perhaps as amusing as it is instructive, but of course, once again, it is only of suggestive value. Nevertheless, it is consistent with the other testimony we have presented in this section in indicating that the visual perceptions of the blind and near-blind may reflect an acuity and accuracy that makes conventional explanations appear strangely contorted.

In any event, our last case is, in our view, our strongest since it is backed up by independent witnesses and various forms of documentation. It concerns a forty-one-year-old woman named Nancy who in September, 1991, entered a hospital in California for what was supposed to be a routine biopsy. The surgical procedure, however, turned out to be anything but routine, and Nancy, who was fully sighted before her hospitalization, ended up losing her sight completely and almost losing her life as well. Her story is both gripping and tragic, but it affords us some extraordinary evidence that near-death vision in the blind is indeed accurate and verifiable.

Because the details in Nancy's story are precisely what make it both valuable and potentially confirmable, we will be paying close attention to them in this account. We begin with some excerpts from our interview with her about certain crucial particulars of her experience. She is being asked about the circumstances of her NDE.

Nancy: [They went into my chest] that morning to do what was supposed to be a very simple, one-cut-of-the-forceps biopsy to determine what the cancer was. They knew it was a very large tumor in my chest. Upon the first cut, the superior vena cava was cut by accident. Then, as a result of panic by everyone involved, it was sewn closed and the surgeon did not realize what he had done. I came out of surgery—the operative report is rather vague, but I went into surgery that morning at 7:30 and came out around 11:30 that morning and went directly into recovery. And of course this was all an accident. I was scheduled to go back to work a day or two afterward and then go through chemotherapy and radiation. I was diagnosed very late because I thought I had injured my shoulder in a roller skating accident in March. And all of the symptoms of my tumor until August and September I attributed to what I thought was the shoulder injury.... So I went into recovery and at some point early in the afternoon, my upper extremities started to swell and turn purple—that is an indication that the blood flow had stopped in the head, or chest, neck, and head. At that point they realized something really bad had happened and they brought me out of recovery and I was already telling people as I was waking, "I'm blind, I'm blind," and everyone thought well, it's a result of the significant swelling in the head. So they brought me out of recovery—I stopped breathing at some point—and...

Interviewer: So you woke up at one point but then stopped breathing after you became conscious?

Nancy: Yes. And was wheeled out of recovery on a stat basis to go down to have an MRI. And as the gurney is coming to the elevator—now this is part of my memory, this is my experience—as it was coming towards an elevator, they slammed into the elevator, like ran into it. There were, like, three people on the left, three people on the right, IVs going, and a black—do you know what an ambu bag is?

Interviewer: No, I don't.

Nancy: An ambu bag looks like a black football. And it is something that instead of being on a respirator or other apparatus, this is something that's manually done. It's put over the nose and mouth and you're forced to breathe. You've probably seen it. And it's called an ambu bag. I remember that.

Interviewer: You were breathing into that?

Nancy: That was forcing me to breathe 'cause I wasn't breathing on my own. And as the gurney hit the elevator, that's when there was a big jolt and it was just like a movie. Just like they say. And everything—my experience is just like what everybody says. I kind of came out of my own body and just like, stepped off of the gurney, off to the side, and stood there, and just watched the whole event.

Interviewer: Could you be specific in terms of what you saw?

Nancy: Yes.

Interviewer: And was it a visual perception?

Nancy: Yes.

Interviewer: And could you tell me the clarity with which you saw, too?

Nancy: Extremely clear. And to this moment it's just like it happened five seconds ago. Or it's happening right now, I can just see the whole thing.

Interviewer: Okay. It would be very helpful if you could be as detailed as possible.

Nancy: Okay, I was on the gurney. I wasn't really aware of what I looked like but as the gurney hit the elevator I stepped out of myself, stood, like, next to the elevator, and was watching. I then looked away from myself on the gurney and looked down the hall about fifteen or twenty feet. And there were two men standing there. One of the men was/is my son's father. I have an eight-and-a-half-year-old son. The other man was my lover at the time. And they were standing there just—just kind of looking. And I thought to myself, "Why aren't they coming up and doing something or saying something? You know, this is probably going to be the last chance they're gonna have to see me." But they didn't. And then the bright light...

Interviewer: Now when you saw them, do you mean the part of you that separated and was standing next to...

Nancy: It was just like being a person standing there. I was just like a person standing there. But nobody could see me.

Interviewer: Do you remember any features that you had, like whether or not you had a body, that sort of thing? Do you remember seeing anything?

Nancy: Of myself? Well, I tend to think that it was just like me, normally looking, standing there. But I wasn't really looking at myself in that state. I, the person standing by the elevator, was looking at me on the gurney.

Interviewer: What did you see when you looked at yourself on the gurney?

Nancy: I saw all the people and the IV and the black ambu bag covering my face and one of those surgical head covers, like when you come out of surgery. And then the mattress, the white sheet, and the white sheet over me. And so I really couldn't see or didn't realize much of what my body looked like....

Interviewer: Did you see anything or anyone else around the area?

Nancy: No, just the people who I could not describe to you. Just the people, like three people on the left of the gurney and three people on the right—staff people. And they were all in a panic. And of course they didn't mean to run into the elevator. You know it was like, you know, wham! And that was like what jolted me. And that started this process. And the two men that were standing there just looked like they were just in shock. And they weren't talking to themselves, to each other—they were just standing there. And they were looking at the gurney, but not making a move. And then the classic white light, bright, the most beautiful light, soothing, comforting just awashing over [me]. And who it was awashing over was me on the gurney. And it was just like what I would consider like a laser beam. That bright and clear and focused. And I started moving toward the light.

At this point Nancy went into the light, and, after being urged to return, she eventually decided to come back. About her physical condition afterward, she had this to add:

Nancy: That's really it. I don't have any other memories. I don't have memories of the elevator doors opening or me getting onto it or anything else. Let me say one more thing, Sharon, I went down to the MRI and they realized what had happened, that the superior vena cava had been sewn closed, sutured shut. At 7:30 that night they went back in. They did not give me much of a chance to make it. They brought in other surgeons, went in, [and] opened up the vena cava. I was already blind and had been since early afternoon as a result, they believe, of the ... optic nerves not getting lubrication simultaneously. No blood flow. And they went back in and they did a bypass of the vena cava, opened it back up, and kept it open, but realized they couldn't get enough of a blood flow. [They] did a bypass and I've got a three inch Goretex graft in my neck all the way down to the superior vena cava. And I spent five days on a respirator not able to talk, being restrained intermittently. And the whole time I was pretty much unconscious as a result of the morphine and them wanting to keep me sedated. They did not paralyze me though. You know they can do that with the drugs. They did not do that.... They didn't start actively trying to bring my eyesight back 'til after I was off the respirator and they realized a) that I was going to live and b) they could talk to me and try to make some sense of things. And it was too late. They brought in people from all over the world to see me and there wasn't anything to do. They tried one thing, using steroids ten times the human dose, and it didn't work.

So, it proved impossible to restore Nancy's sight, as a result of which she remains completely blind to this day because of this medical mishap.

This, then, is Nancy's account of her experience and the circumstances leading up to and following it. But we also have been able to interview the two men she claims to have seen while out of body—her lover and the father of her child—and Nancy has also furnished us with her medical records, so we have a great deal of information on the basis of which to compare Nancy's narrative to other independent versions of the events surrounding her experience. First, her medical records essentially confirm the external aspects of her biopsy and subsequent reparative surgery. Second, the most helpful corroborative testimony came from her lover at the time, Leon, whom we interviewed on two separate occasions. Third, he also sent us copies of all the notes he had made at the time as well as copies of Nancy's initial attempts, shortly after her surgery, to write that she had lost her sight. We therefore will continue with some copious excerpts from our principal interview with Leon on April 2, 1995. As will be apparent, his account is in substantial agreement with Nancy's. In effect, in his interview, he tells the same story she does, only from his perspective.

Leon: I had to drive down about an hour to pick her up and take her into the hospital. It must have been around 6 o'clock in the morning. Somewhere around there. I'm not quite sure of the time. She went in—I think about 7 o'clock she went and did the biopsy. I waited in the waiting room until around—I waited for several hours and I knew it was only supposed to be an hour procedure, and I got very, very concerned and kept asking, "What is going on?" No one would answer me. Finally, probably about five hours after she went in the surgeon came out—almost six hours—must have been about one o'clock in the afternoon—he came out and took me to another room and told me what had happened to her and that they didn't know what was going on. There was just a lot of vague information that I had. So I became extremely concerned.... I probably didn't see her again until around 4 o'clock in the afternoon, I think. And when I saw her first, it was a fluke. I was in the hallway by the surgery and she was coming out and I could tell it was her. They were kind of rushing her out.

Interviewer: Rushing her out of where?

Leon: Of the surgery suite where she had been in the recovery area, I think. And I saw these people coming out. I saw people wheeling a gurney. I saw about four or five people with her, and I looked and I said, "God, it looks like Nancy," but her face and her upper torso were really swollen about twice the size it should have been. At that point I looked and I said, "Nancy, Nancy," and they just— she didn't know, I mean. She was out of it. And they told me they were taking her down for an angiogram.

Interviewer: Who told you that?

Leon: I believe a nurse did. I'm not quite sure. I think I was still in a state of shock. I mean, it had been a long day for me. You're expecting an hour procedure and here it is, approximately ten hours later and you don't have very many answers. I believe a nurse did. I know I asked. And I think Dick [the father of Nancy's child] was there at the same time. I think he and I were talking in the hallway.

Interviewer: Do you know how far you were from Nancy?

Leon: When I first saw her she was probably, maybe about one hundred feet and then she went right by us. I was probably no more than three to five feet away from her. And I believe Dick was right next to me as well.

Interviewer: And do you know how they took her out? She was on the gurney?

Leon: She was on the gurney. There were IVs.... I'm not sure—I think she had some sort of a breathing apparatus. I'm not sure if it was an ambu bag or what it was.

Interviewer: And then where did they take her?

Leon: They took her downstairs to do an angiogram.

Interviewer: How?

Leon: They took her down in the gurney in the service elevator. They didn't take her in a regular elevator. They took her around the corner to the service elevator.

Interviewer: And did you see that whole process?

Leon: Yes, I did.

Interviewer: Did you see her go into the elevator?

Leon: Yes, I did because I walked around to watch her enter the elevator.

Interviewer: Was there any disturbance that you remember in getting her into the elevator?

Leon: I think there was a real sense of urgency on the staff. I've worked in hospital emergency rooms as well and I can really relate to that. I think somebody was, like, trying to get into the elevator at the same time and there was some sort of a "Oh, I can't get in, let's move this over a little bit," kind of adjusting before they could get her into the elevator. But it was very swift.

Interviewer: Did you have a good look at her face?

Leon: Yeah, it really kind of shocked me. She was just really swollen. She was totally unrecognizable. I mean, I knew it was her but—you know, I was a medic in Vietnam and it was just like seeing a body after a day after they get bloated. It was the same kind of look.

Here, as we have already indicated, it is obvious that Leon's account squares with Nancy's in virtually every significant respect, particularly in regard to his verification that he and Dick were indeed standing in the hallway just as Nancy had perceived them. This was so despite the fact that Leon was very worried about her condition at the time and could scarcely recognize her because of her edema when he did see her. Yet, despite his evident state of shock during this incident, his interview appears to corroborate her story, as much as any external witness could be expected to. (25)

The account furnished to us by Dick, the father of Nancy's child, also generally accords with the recall of both Nancy and Leon, although he said several times during our interview that his memory was hazy and that he couldn't vouch for all the details.

As for Nancy's sight status, we have heard her say that she was already blind at the time of her experience, so she couldn't possibly have seen these men with her physical eyes. Yet, we do not have any direct verification of this statement from her medical records where the first indication of her blindness doesn't occur until 8 a.m. on October 2, two days *after* her surgery. (There is, however, a handwritten note of Leon's the day before, made at 1:55 p.m., referring to a conversation with Nancy's anesthesiologist who said, according to Leon, that her eyesight was affected by "the swelling but would reverse itself when the swelling goes down.") These small but crucial discrepancies lead us directly to the question of when precisely Nancy *did* forfeit her sight. We need to determine with as much certainty as we can whether Nancy was in fact blind at the time of the gurney incident. Accordingly, we naturally asked Leon to tell us what he could recall about this matter.

Interviewer: Do you know whether she had lost her vision before she was taken into the elevator?

Leon: I did not know that. We did not know that until she was in the ICU and I still have her notes that she wrote—tried to write—which said "I can't see." [They actually read, "lost sight."]

Interviewer: And when did she write those notes?

Leon: Let me see. She had tubes every which way.... This was after she came back from the angiogram and they brought her into the ICU. They gave her a private room in the ICU. I'm trying to remember when that was. I think that was like—it's real cloudy—it was probably within 24 hours from the time she walked into the surgery. [His notes show that her first attempt to write that she had lost her sight took place at 9:30 p.m. of September 30th, the same day as her operation.]

Interviewer: That was the first time you were aware that she was blind?

Leon: That we were all aware. That she said, "I can't see."

Interviewer: So you don't know whether she was blind before that time?

Leon: No. You mean before she went down for the angiogram?

Interviewer: Exactly.

Leon: No. Nobody knew. I mean, I didn't know. I don't think the physicians knew either. They just knew that she was in bad shape. In terms of her blindness, we didn't know until—I think everyone was just as surprised as I was.

Nancy herself, of course, claims that when she awoke from the anesthetic, she was already shouting that she was blind and later told us her blindness "was not at all a slow process.... It seems like there was never any diminution in my sight—it was an all-or-nothing thing."

Is it medically possible for Nancy to have lost her sight so quickly following her operation? According to our own ophthalmological consultant, apparently it is. In his view, after a major occlusion of the sort that Nancy experienced, damage to the optic nerve could occur in minutes, causing complete cortical blindness. In Nancy's case, we know from Leon's notes and her medical records that at least six hours, and probably more, had passed from the time her superior vena cava was cut until she was wheeled on that gurney in the presence of Leon and Dick.

Nancy's assertion that she was blind at that moment was true and that she couldn't have seen these men through normal vision. But even if she *had* retained some residual physical vision at this time, having the ambu bag on her head, as we discovered when we examined this device ourselves, would have prevented the kind of lateral vision necessary to see them from her supine position, to say nothing of the obstructive shield provided by the attendants surrounding her gurney.

Thus, we conclude that in all probability there was no possibility for Nancy to see what she did with her physical eyes which, in any event, were almost surely sightless by that time. Yet, she did see, and, as the corroborative testimony we have provided shows, she apparently saw truly.

The question of course is *how?* And not only how did Nancy see, but how do *any* of the blind persons whose narratives we have considered in this lengthy presentation of the findings of this study see what they certainly cannot possibly be seeing physically? Our findings in this chapter only establish a reasonable case that these visions are factually accurate, and not just some kind of fabrication, reconstruction, lucky guess or fantasy, but they leave unexplained the paradox of our discovery that, after all, the rumors some of us have been hearing all these years, that the blind can actually see during their NDEs, appear to be true. Whether and how this can be so is the mystery we must next be prepared to probe, and, if possible, to solve.

Chapter Six

Addressing the Paradox:
How Do the Blind See?

An overview of our findings

Since we have examined in detail so many case histories and quoted so extensively from our interviews, it will be helpful to summarize our principal findings here at the outset before tackling the perplexing and difficult questions we posed at the end of the last chapter. To do so, we will return to the three issues this study was designed to probe, and which we first presented toward the close of our opening chapter dealing with the evidence prior to this study for the paradox of apparent sight in the blind.

The first of these was to determine whether blind persons do report NDEs and, if they do, whether they are the same as or different from those of sighted persons. Our findings here were unequivocal in the affirmative. There is no question that NDEs in the blind do occur and, furthermore, that they take the same general form and are comprised of the very same elements that define the NDEs of sighted individuals. Moreover, this generalization appears to hold across all three categories of blindness that were represented in this study: those blind from birth, the adventitiously blind, and the severely visually impaired.

The second issue, and the one that was the driving force of this study, was of course whether the blind claim to have visual impressions during their NDEs or OBEs. On this point, too, our data were conclusive. Overall, 80% of our respondents reported these claims, most of them in the language of unhesitating declaration, even when they may have been surprised, or even stunned, by the unexpected discovery that they could in fact see. Like sighted experiencers, our blind respondents described to us both perceptions of this world as well as otherworldly scenes, often in fulsome, fine-grained detail, and sometimes with a sense of extremely sharp, even subjectively perfect, acuity.

The last issue hinged on the second, and that had to do with attempting to corroborate these claims of sight—at least for perceptions of the natural world—in an effort to show that they represented something other than fantasies or hallucinations. This was the weakest part of our study since for a variety of methodological reasons it was often not possible to locate relevant witnesses or gain access to potentially helpful documentation. Nevertheless, we did present some cases that were highly suggestive that these claims are indeed authentic and not explicable by conventional means, and at least one case where independent evidence did corroborate in every critical respect the testimony provided by a blind patient.

Some supplementary cases

Before moving on to a consideration of possible interpretations of our findings, we would like to take a moment to furnish some information about a couple of relevant cases that came to our attention following the conclusion of our study when one of us (K.R.) was on a lecture tour in Australia during March, 1996. At that time, two NDErs, one partially sighted, the other adventitiously blind, made themselves known and were informally interviewed. Each subsequently wrote us a letter describing the circumstances and nature of their NDEs, and in what follows we will be quoting a bit from these documents.

The first individual, Jeff van Geelan, was actually present during a lecture, and at the intermission came up to share his own story privately, though he subsequently disclosed it briefly to the audience as a whole. We do not know his exact age, but he appeared to be about sixty. Here are the particulars that make his experience of interest.

Jeff is completely blind in his right eye and has limited vision in the other. On November 12, 1987, Jeff suffered a heart attack and stroke and, according to his letter, was without a heartbeat for approximately three-and-a-half minutes. During that time, he had a classic, radiant NDE during which, he says, "I started to see and notice things." He was aware, for example, of lifting out of his physical body, passing with increasing speed through a silver and light-blue cylinder and eventually found himself "traveling at an incredible pace through this tunnel at the end of which I saw a great white light" following which he returned to his body.

What makes Jeff's NDE of special interest to us, however, is that, as he said during our private chat at the lecture, he realized subsequently that during his NDE he could see perfectly and with unaccustomed binocular vision. This revelation, as he put it in his letter, "hit me like a jolt." In life, he had long grown used to his restricted field of vision on his right side, but as he wrote us:

> The sudden awareness of this handicap was put in front of me when I came back from my NDE when I opened my eyes and discovered that the arc of sight was reduced from the previous moment: I HAD SEEN THE PATH TO AND THROUGH THE TUNNEL THROUGH BOTH MY EYES! [Capitalization in the original.]

The second person is a forty-year-old woman, Judith Killen, who became totally blind at the age of two-and-a-half as a result of bilateral retinoblastomas. When she was eleven, she had a severe asthma attack at night and nearly died.

After a physician was called in, he gave her an injection and Judith relaxed, feeling very peaceful after her long struggle to gain her breath. Suddenly:

> I was shocked to notice that I, my soul or spirit, was separate from the body, looking down at it from the corner of the ceiling. My body appeared as its size and shape lying face up on my bed. I was not aware of any particular features, just the form of my body, lying still.... I was aware of the distance between my soul and my body form on the bed. Also, I think this was the first time I had seen my body, as another person might detachedly see someone.

During this time, as Judith was later to learn, she actually was close to death, as her physician subsequently revealed to her. He had rushed back into her room to find she had in fact lapsed into another and even more severe asthmatic spasm in consequence of which she had to be rushed to a nearby hospital for oxygen.

Although not mentioned in her letter, according to notes taken during a telephone interview with Judith, what she actually saw [she used that verb] was more of an "outline" of her body, "an image of me on the bed." Her language here is especially noteworthy because it appears to coincide almost exactly with that of one of our own respondents, Marilyn, whose case we previously cited in connection with the difficulty our interviewees sometimes expressed about how to characterize the nature of their perception of their physical body while seemingly hovering above it.

In any event, these two Australian cases are obviously highly consistent with the overall findings of this study and thus add in a small but still significant way to the potential generalizability of our discoveries about the nature of NDEs and visual processing in the blind.

Some possible explanations for apparent sight in the blind

With this summary of our findings, supplemented by these additional Australian cases, we are now ready to explore the questions of central interest to us. The simplest way to frame the issue might be to ask, "How is it that the blind can see during these experiences?" But, however natural it might be to put the question in this form, doing so implies we have already concluded that we can reasonably infer from our data that the blind do in fact see. That is certainly possible, perhaps even plausible, but clearly not all readers would be prepared to concede the point. Indeed, we have already implied that from an epistemological point of view, it might be better to rephrase our basic question as: "If it can legitimately be said that the blind *in some sense* do see, in precisely *what sense* would that be?" Putting the question in this way, then, leaves open the issue of the nature of apparent sight in the blind. However, even before we can properly address *this* question, there is plainly still another one that must exert a prior claim on our attention, and that is: "Might there not be non-retinal-based mechanisms that could in principle account for the results of this study and thus demonstrate that vision in the blind is indeed only apparent and not actual?"

Thus, by a series of interrogative declensions, we find ourselves facing first the possibility of various alternative explanations that would enable us to avoid having to posit some kind of eyeless vision to subsume our findings. And, clearly, it makes sense that before resorting to possible unconventional theories such as those rooted in New Paradigm science or even esoteric thought to interpret our findings, we must first make sure that no already recognized natural or prosaic mechanism can provide a superior or more parsimonious explanation. Accordingly, we begin by considering some of the possible contenders in this category for explanatory honors.

The dream hypothesis

One fairly obvious possibility here that has often been advanced in connection with the NDEs (and OBEs) of sighted persons is that this experience is some kind of a dream, perhaps a lucid or exceptionally vivid dream, which has such realistic properties that it is easily misinterpreted and thus given an ontological status it doesn't deserve.

To begin to evaluate this hypothesis, we first need to inquire into what is known about normal oneiric processes in the blind. Fortunately, there has been a great deal of research devoted to the dreams of the blind, some of it going back more than a hundred years. As a result of all these investigations, certain generalizations about the presence of visual imagery in dreams appear to stand up quite well. Among these "empirical cornerstones" (as summarized in Kirtley [1975]) are the following: 1) There are no visual images in the dreams of the congenitally blind; 2) Individuals blinded before the age of five also tend not to have visual imagery; 3) Those who become sightless between the age of five and seven may or may not retain visual imagery; 4) Most persons who lose their sight after age 7 do retain visual imagery, although its clarity tends to fade with time.

In addition, various researchers have found that audition tends to be the primary sense involved in dreams of the blind, with tactile and kinesthetic elements next (Kirtley, 1975).

In our interviews, we routinely asked our respondents about the nature of their dreams, and what we found in our sample accords with the generalizations just described. In addition, however, and particularly pertinent to the hypothesis under consideration, our respondents usually went on to say that not only were their NDEs unlike their usual dreams, but they stood out as radically different, precisely because they contained visual imagery, whereas their dreams had always lacked this element. Vicki, one of our NDErs blind from birth, provides a good case in point:

Interviewer: How would you compare your dreams to your NDEs?

Vicki: No similarity, no similarity at all.

Interviewer: Do you have any kind of visual perception in your dreams?

Vicki: Nothing. No color, no sight of any sort, no shadows, no light, no nothing.

Interviewer: What kinds of perceptions are you aware of in your typical dreams?

Vicki: Taste—I have a lot of eating dreams [laughs]. And I have dreams when I'm playing the piano and singing, which I do for a living, anyway. I have dreams in which I touch things.... I taste things, touch things, hear things, and smell things—that's it.

Interviewer: And no visual perceptions?

Vicki: No.

Interviewer: So that what you experienced during your NDE was quite different from your dreams?

Vicki: Yeah, because there's no visual impression at all in any dream that I have.

Brad, another of our NDErs who, like Vicki, was blind from birth, also made comments in this connection that echoed Vicki's.

Brad: Generally—except for this one near-death experience—my dreams have had the very same consciousness ... as I've had in my waking hours. That would be all my senses function, especially my sense of hearing and my sense of touch, but all the other senses function, except vision. In my dreams, I have no visual perceptions at all.

And our other respondents tend to speak along similar lines as these representative quotes will demonstrate:

1. Interviewer: When you dream, do you dream in visual perception?

Respondent: No.

Interviewer: In conversation?

Respondent: I dream like I am with you now or in the living room with my husband or I see light and dark like I do now.

Interviewer: But it's in the same way that you perceive things in your daily life? That's the same state or quality of your dreams?

Respondent: Yeah.

Interviewer: So these near-death experiences are, as far as you can tell or remember, the only times when you've actually had clear sight perception?

Respondent: Yeah, it's weird.

2. I don't usually dream in visual images. Usually, my dreams are either tactile or auditory, and I usually dream the kind of dreams philosophers have—discussion (laughs).

3. I don't feel like it [his NDE] was anything like any dream I ever had.

4. Interviewer: Are your dreams different than either the hallucinations you had while taking prescription medicine or the OBE?
Respondent: Oh yeah.
Interviewer: How are they different from the OBE?
Respondent: The OBE was really peaceful and I just felt I had a great intense rush of peace and love. And my dreams aren't like that.

5. Interviewer: In terms of what you see in your dreams, is it anything like what you saw in the operating room?
Respondent: No, it's about everyday life. It has nothing to do with the hospital [i.e., her experience while in the hospital].... I do remember being lifted up, though. I'll probably remember that for the rest of my life.

These excerpts make it abundantly clear that from our respondents' point of view, the NDE, especially its visual aspect, has nothing in common with their usual dreams. It is instead something *sui generis,* and not to be conflated with dreams. Since there is no support whatever from our interviews for the dream hypothesis of NDEs, we may confidently reject it as a potential explanation for our findings.

Retrospective reconstruction

Another possibility, at least for the kind of visual perceptions respondents report during the out-of-body phase of NDEs, is that individuals are not really seeing at that time, but talking afterward *as if* they did. Instead, according to this hypothesis, they have actually *reconstructed* a plausible account—after the fact—of what might be expected to have happened while they were close to death, although they may sincerely (but erroneously) believe that they witnessed it at the time. From a combination of prior expectations, familiarity with hospital routines, overheard conversations, or other sensory cues at the time, information gleaned afterward or even simply by lucky guesses, it might be possible for an NDEr to imaginatively construct a pictorial representation of events during an NDE. Thus, this hypothesis would contend that what *appears* to be vision is in reality a product of the mind's inventiveness, viz., its ability to create mental imagery that is misconstrued as actual vision.

The chief proponent of this hypothesis is the English parapsychologist, Susan Blackmore (1993) who uses it chiefly to discount some of the pioneering work by the cardiologist, Michael Sabom (1982) in his study of apparently veridical—but seemingly impossible—visual perception in a sample of NDErs. In discussing, for example, how a patient could unconsciously use auditory information available during an operation, Blackmore indicates how naturally such a false representation could be generated:

> It does not take much information from such sounds for a person to piece together a very convincing and realistic visual impression of what is going on. This will provide the best model they

have and seem perfectly real. They may have no idea that the model was constructed primarily from things that they have heard.... It is very hard to assess just how much information any patient would have available. We can only remember the general point that people who appear unconscious may still be aware of some of the things going on around them and they can easily build these up into a good visual picture of what was happening. (Blackmore, 1993, pp. 124-125)

Blackmore's reasoning is logical and her hypothesis has a certain plausibility, but we have not been able to find strong support for it among our interviewees. That is not to say, however, that we have found none. There is one—but *only* one—of our sample of thirty-one respondents who gave voice to this notion. But even here, as we shall later see, it was merely one of a number of explicit *hypotheses* this person considered in an attempt to understand what had happened to him, and, at that, he only mentions it as a logical possibility; he doesn't endorse it or claim it was necessarily true for him. At this point in his interview, he simply says:

Yeah, it might have just been a consolidation of the other perceptions, the sound and the touch and just my mental watching putting two and two together, coming up with an image of what was going on and then I was imagining in my mind. It could've been that. But I can't say for sure that it was merely that. But it was a visual perception, it was not like any state of mind I've ever experienced before.

But arrayed against this hypothesis are a number of inconvenient facts from this study and other research. First, although it obviously cannot be ruled out *a priori* in every case, it is at least noteworthy that no other respondent apart from the one just cited seems to have entertained it. As a result, there is no particular reason to believe that it necessarily could have played a role in most or even some of our cases. And when one considers its obvious *post hoc* quality (i.e., "well, it just *might have* been the case," etc.) and its virtually built-in nondisconfirmable nature, the almost complete lack of direct evidence in its behalf is particularly telling.

Second, this hypothesis clearly founders when it comes to accounting for instances when *unusual* objects (i.e, ones that could not easily have been predicted or otherwise anticipated) are described by the blind. For instance, how could this notion explain Frank's correctly identifying the design and color of his tie, when that information had apparently not been disclosed to him? Or Pat's accurate detection of (for her) the novel features of her friend's ceiling? Nor does it account for cases of apparently veridical perceptions *at a distance,* such as Carla's of her step-father's nurse's name tag or Cheryl's of her sick friend in another's home. Also, the many minute particulars described by our respondents, such as the detailed description given by Brad of the texture of the snow he claims to have seen, would not be expected on the basis of a hypothesis of *generalized* retrospective reconstruction.

Third, even if this hypothesis were able to assimilate such facts, it is obvious that it is completely impotent when it comes to accounting for the otherworldly segment of NDEs, which is especially clear in visual form for many of our respondents, as we have noted. These visions accord very well with those of sighted NDErs and can hardly be based on environmental cues, whether contemporary with or subsequent to the NDE. Moreover, in regard to a possible expectational effect, it should be remembered that some of these experiences, such as Vicki's and Brad's, actually took place even *before* the advent of modern NDE studies, which began with the publication of Raymond Moody's book, *Life after Life,* in 1975. So, even if expectation were a factor, this hypothesis could not in itself explain all of the features consistently mentioned by our blind NDErs.

Finally, Sabom himself, when he came to interpret his findings from the study in which veridical information was seemingly obtained by his patients during the out-of-body phase of their NDEs, did in fact carefully examine the possible role of precisely the kind of external factors Blackmore wants to implicate. His conclusion, which is amply supported by explicit reference to significant counter-examples in his report, reads:

> Thus, we have attempted to explain the apparent accuracy of the[se] ... NDEs by prior general knowledge, by information passed on by another individual, and by physical perception of sight and sound during semiconsciousness. None of these possibilities have been found to be plausible explanations. (Sabom, 1982, p. 115)

In this connection, it is also relevant to note that the late D. Scott Rogo (1989), in an independent assessment of this hypothesis, based on both Sabom's findings and Blackmore's arguments, came to the same conclusion.

On the basis of all the foregoing considerations, we find scant evidence in favor of this hypothesis, and a number of cogent reasons not only to reject it, but to be tempted to regard it almost as a kind of all-purpose refuge for the skeptically-minded, rather like the Super-ESP hypothesis in parapsychology (26), which in principle is always capable of explaining away in a pseudo-scientific fashion findings that threaten to disturb prevailing ideas of the possible.

Blindsight

In the early 1970s, Lawrence Weiskrantz began to study a curious phenomenon he was later to call "blindsight" (Weiskrantz, 1986) in which patients suffering from extensive cortical blindness appeared to be able to "see." In his experiments, for example, Weiskrantz was able to show that in the absence of any visual sensation, patients, if asked to reach for a nearby object about whose exact location they were ignorant, tended to move in the right direction. Furthermore, when asked to grasp objects the nature of which was not disclosed to them beforehand, their hands tended spontaneously to assume the appropriate form necessary to hold the object. Weiskrantz's work has since been replicated by others (e.g., Humphrey, 1993) and the phenomenon has even been found in monkeys after extirpation of the visual cortex.

The neuroscientists who have been investigating or writing about this seemingly baffling condition (e.g., Newman, 1997; Stoerig, Cowey & Goebel, 1998; Weiskrantz, 1986, 1996, 1997) tend to posit that there are portions of the brain, originating in the brain stem, that relay visual inputs to cortical areas *outside of* the visual cortex. Hypothetically, these inputs provide the neural basis for a type of perception without conscious vision. In effect, they create a condition that is analogous to the performance of split brain patients for whom a stimulus projected to one side of the brain may be behaviorally acknowledged but remain linguistically inaccessible.

This kind of explanation, however, is still controversial and admittedly speculative (Newman, 1997, p. 57), but no matter how this phenomenon may ultimately be accounted for, we still must turn to the question of its relevance here. Accordingly we must ask whether it is possible that what our respondents report is actually a form of blindsight.

Further scrutiny of the results of research into blindsight shows very quickly that, although it seems to be a legitimate form of perception, it can by no means account for our findings. First of all, patients manifesting the effect typically cannot verbally describe the object they are alleged to see, unlike our respondents who, as we have noted, were usually certain about what they saw and could describe it often without hesitation. In fact, a cortically blind patient, even when his or her object identification exceeds chance levels, believes that it is largely the result of pure guesswork. Such uncertainties were not characteristic of our respondents. Second, even when performance is better than chance would allow, patients still make many errors, even the best of them (Humphrey, 1993). While we cannot of course provide an overall figure of accuracy of object identification in our study, it is not obvious from our findings, in regard to reports of visual perception in those portions of the environmental visual field where attention was focused, that errors were made. Finally, and perhaps most crucially of all, blindsight patients, unlike our respondents, do not claim that they can "see" in any sense. As Humphrey puts it, "Certainly the patient says he does not have visual sensation.... Rather he says, 'I don't know anything at all—but if you tell me I'm getting it right I have to take your word for it (p. 90).'" This kind of statement is simply not found in the testimony of our respondents who, on the contrary, are often convinced that they have somehow seen what they report.

Thus, the blindsight phenomenon, however fascinating it may be in its own right, cannot begin to explain our findings. Indeed, the term itself seems to be a bit of an unintentional misnomer since in such patients there is not any conscious sense of visual perception at all.

Skin-based vision

The idea that we may have a kind of eyeless visual back-up system based on dermal sensitivity is an old one, although at first blush the notion may seem preposterous. Yet, when one thinks about it for a moment, the retina itself is just a specialized piece of skin, which through evolution has come to be the "vision specialist" for the body. Therefore, it is certainly conceivable that in our skin itself there might be a residual basis for visual detection which has simply atrophied and become non-functional through disuse, like a vestigial organ.

That this supposition is not merely speculative but based in solid modern scientific reasoning is evident in the work of such well-known researchers as Paul Bach-y-Rita, a physician who for many years has specialized in the study of sensory substitution mechanisms and whose practical inventions along these lines we will be discussing shortly. In his ground-breaking book, *Brain Mechanisms in Sensory Substitution* (1972), he outlines the rationale for postulating a kind of skin-based vision:

> The skin shows a number of functional similarities to the retina in its capacity to mediate information. Large parts of the body surface are relatively flat, and the receptor surfaces of the skin and retina are capable of mediating displays in two spatial dimensions as well as having the potential for

temporal integration.... In addition, there is evidence that the skin normally functions as an exteroceptor at least in a limited sense; to some extent both vibration and temperature changes can be felt at a distance.... The skin receptor matrix has been shown capable of mediating three-dimensional spatial information in such a way that the central nervous system can analyze this information in terms usually considered "visual". (pp. 11-12)

But is this really a type of vision? Obviously, not as we are accustomed to thinking about it, but conceptually it is no different from retina-mediated vision, as Bach-y-Rita (1972) makes clear:

If a subject without functioning eyes can perceive detailed visual information in space, correctly locate it subjectively, and respond to it in a manner comparable to the response of a normally sighted person, I feel justified in applying the term "vision". (pp. ix-x)

So much for theory. But where, one might ask, is the empirical data to support it? Let's look into this question now in an effort to see whether a theory of skin-based vision might provide a tenable alternative explanation for the findings of this study.

The pioneer researcher in this field seems to have been a French scientist by the name of Jules Romains. (27) In 1920, he published a now nearly forgotten book called *La Vision Extra-Rétinienne et la Sens Paroptique,* which described his experiments in skin-based perception. (In 1924, an English translation of his book became available under the title of *Eyeless Sight: A Study of Extra-Retinal*

Vision and the Paroptic Sense.) A brief overview of his aims, methods and findings follows.

His general purpose was to determine if individuals could "see" without the use of their eyes. To investigate this possibility, he first blindfolded his subjects in such a way as to ensure that no light could penetrate their eyes. He then ran them through a series of experiments to assess their visual capabilities under these conditions. In some, he would present them with a newspaper and ask them to "read" the headlines. In others, he would ask his subjects to "read" a set of numbers. In still others, as in modern blindsight experiments, he would invite them to describe an object he placed in front (or sometimes) behind them. Or he might ask his subjects to identify the colors of objects or to distinguish the colors of papers under glass.

In general, and quite astonishingly, Romains reports that his subjects performed remarkably well, far exceeding what would have been possible by chance. Furthermore, these experiments were witnessed by many observers, some of them quite eminent, and therefore do not depend solely on his own word. Romains found, however, that several conditions had to be met in order for these tests to be successful or at least to affect the probability of correct identification. First, even though the subjects were blindfolded, light had to be present in the room for them to be able to "see." Second, his subjects could not perceive the object or "read" the number or letters on a paper when an opaque screen or door was placed between them and the object. Finally, the greater the area of the skin actually exposed, the more subjects tended to be accurate in their descriptions.

Romains developed some elaborate theories to explain his findings, which we do not have to concern ourselves with here, but however intriguing his discoveries were, they do not seem to have much bearing on what we found in our study. There are several distinct reasons for this conclusion. To begin with, we have just noted that in Romains' experiments, shielding the object from view prevented it from being "seen." Yet, in our study, even the presence of walls or ceilings proved to be no impediment to our respondents' apparent vision, as cases such as Vicki's, Brad's, Carla's and Cheryl's, among others, attest. In addition, whereas Romains found that the degree of skin exposure was directly related to accuracy of perception, there was no evidence of that in our study, and in fact some evidence that would contravene it. Remember, for instance, that in some of our cases the respondent's body was covered with bed sheets or was clothed at the time of an NDE or OBE, yet vision seemed to occur without difficulty. Most telling of all, however, is that Romains' subjects generally took a long time to achieve whatever degree of visual accuracy they did demonstrate. Indeed throughout his book, Romains frequently comments that the kind of eyeless vision he obtained from his subjects was piecemeal, gradual, with the elements of perception coming together slowly, as a result of laborious effort, at least at the beginning. Eyeless vision, he states, is successive, a matter of trial-and-error, and tends at first to be able to discern only objects near at hand. Obviously, in our study, visual perception seemed to be immediate, unlearned, and was not restricted to objects close to the individual. Therefore we conclude, as we did with the later experiments in blindsight, that Romains' findings, even if valid, have no relevance for ours and must depend on entirely different mechanisms.

More than half a century after Romains' book had been published—only to evoke a predictably skeptical or even outrightly dismissive response—another French investigator, Yvonne Duplessis (1975), tried to replicate and extend some of Romains' work. In her case, however, she was especially interested in what she called "dermo-optic" sensitivity and attempted to determine whether blind or partially blind subjects could detect color by this means. To test this, she would present to adventitiously blind or blindfolded subjects differently colored objects and ask them to try to identify the colors. Sometimes subjects were permitted to run their hands over these objects, while in other experiments they would be placed at a distance or would be separated by glass or an opaque screen.

In general, colors were recognized at better than chance levels, apparently, according to Duplessis, because of the thermal or tactile quality they evoked. For example, blue "felt" cool whereas red "felt" more rugged and hot, while green tended to give off a cold sensation and seemed "smooth." (28) As with Romains' findings, there were some limiting conditions: Subjects had to be mentally well and in excellent health to perform well. If they were ill, for example, they did badly. And these tests were fatiguing and appeared to require tremendous concentration.

Here again, we see that Duplessis' work, though of some intrinsic interest, sheds no light on ours. Unlike our respondents, the colors reported by her subjects were not seen so much as they were "felt." And obviously, by definition, all of our NDErs were very ill at the time of their experiences, and hardly in a position to concentrate on objects close at hand.

A few years later, another researcher, Jacobo Grinberg-Zylberbaum (1983) proposed a theory of what he called "extraocular vision" based on some novel experiments of his own. According to him, children under the age of fifteen can "see" without using their eyes if they are given even brief training in yogic methods of meditation and visualization. To demonstrate this proposition, Grinberg-Zylberbaum did a study involving nineteen children between the ages of five and thirteen.

After receiving one to three training sessions in meditation and visualization, these children were blindfolded and then shown a photograph, which they were allowed to touch. In the beginning, they were given feedback to help them learn this kind of "extraocular vision" until they became proficient. Then the children would be shown objects or pictures or even text and asked to describe or "read" what was being presented to them without touch being permitted.

With few exceptions, Grinberg-Zylberbaum found that these children came to perform very well indeed, accurately describing colors and objects, and even being able to read complete words (or identify letters in the case of foreign words)—and all, apparently, without the use of the eyes or other external cues.

Although there are some reasons to be concerned about the methodological rigor of this study and to wonder if it could be independently replicated, these findings, if valid, would seem at first blush to have some direct implications for our own. However, once again, it will be obvious both on reflection and a closer examination of Grinberg-Zylberbaum's study, that his ideas and findings about extraocular vision can't accommodate our data.

First, this researcher himself says that "it is difficult to evoke the phenomenon [of extraocular vision] after an age of about 15 years" (Grinberg-Zylberbaum, 1983, p. 151), which clearly exempts the overwhelming majority of our respondents who were older than this when they had their NDEs or OBEs. Second, few of these persons, even if they had their experiences before the age of fifteen, had the necessary training in meditation and visualization which, according to Grinberg-Zylberbaum makes it possible to "see" in this fashion. And, as we have noted before, the very fact that it takes a while even to learn this type of perception—again assuming it is a true phenomenon— means that it is a substantially different modality from that which is responsible for the immediate vision of our experiencers.

Finally, we come—and return to—the work of Bach-y-Rita and others who have developed an ingenious technique called the Tactile Vision Substitution System (TVSS) by which a type of vision can occur without the use of the eyes (Bach-y-Rita, Scadden & Collins, 1975). In a nutshell, this involves using the skin as a channel for pictorial information by converting optical images into a tactile display. This system electronically transforms images from a closed-circuit television camera, which is attached to the subject's head, into tactile stimulation on a ten-inch-square region of the subject's back. Each point stimulated on the skin in effect represents one small segment of the pictorial image in the same way a newspaper photograph is comprised of an array of individual dots.

The subjects, who are often blind, undergo a training period of anywhere from 10 to 40 hours. And TVSS has proven successful, to a degree at least, in teaching the blind to "see" by this method. For instance, with only a few hours' training, subjects were able to learn to recognize a variety of common objects, such as a telephone, a cup, and a toy horse. After about 30 hours of training, some of them were able to make complex pattern discriminations and, with more training, even to identify the faces of some of the laboratory staff. More interesting still, with sufficient training, subjects said that they were perceiving objects as "out there" in a three-dimensional space, presumably much as normally sighted persons would.

The work of Bach-y-Rita and his colleagues is fascinating, and certainly of considerable practical importance as a teaching device for the blind, but, again, it fails to provide a model for the kind of vision reported by our respondents. For one thing, the images seen via TVSS do not occur in real time. That is, there is a delay in the processing of the information by the subject because typically he or she will have to make several scans with the camera before the tactile stimulations afford a recognizable image. The perception reported by our respondents, as we have already mentioned several times now, is *immediate* like normal vision. For another, TVSS is a *training* device, and, obviously, that training takes time—lots of it. For example, in a telephone interview we conducted with Bach-y-Rita on March 30, 1995, he conceded that though in some instances it might be faster, it generally takes up to two hundred hours for a subject to learn face recognition. Our respondents, however, seemed to require *zero* time for this, even those who were blind from birth.

Thus, in all these methods of skin-based vision we see that, although there may be evidence that the skin is indeed a medium for a kind of sight, it a*lways* takes a while—often a great while—to learn, and that fact alone disqualifies all of these theories as a possible explanatory vehicle for our results. Furthermore, as we have seen in connection with each of these methods, there are always one or more additional specific reasons to reject these theories as alternative explanations. In short, none of them is capable of subsuming our findings. Eyeless vision trainees may be having some kind of genuine perceptional experience, but it does not accord with the kind of vision reported by our respondents.

The necessary rejection of these theories also implies that similar views, such as Krishnan's (1983), which contend that the vision reported in NDEs and OBEs may be a function of some kind of physical mechanism, however obscure, are without support. For instance, Krishnan's position, as we have seen, requires that congenitally blind persons, on seeing for the first time, have inchoate perception, as do those whose sight is restored through an operation (Gregory, 1966, Sacks, 1993, Senden, 1960; Valvo, 1971). But, clearly, that is not the case. The brief surprise or disorientation a blind NDEr may experience, when confronted with visual impressions and before adjusting to them, does not begin to compare with the hours of training that a newly sighted individual needs to undergo in order to transform visual information into meaningful patterns. Relatively speaking, then, sight is virtually immediate in our blind NDErs, and although there may be some confusion over the *fact* of sight and uncertainty about color, object perception seems stable from the outset. Moreover, when never-before-seeing NDErs find themselves in the transcendental portions of their experience, some of them remark that seeing was perfectly natural in that state—it was if they could *always* see. What kind of mechanism could explain that baffling fact is, to us, *really* obscure. In any event, the hypothesis that it might be rooted in some kind of skin-based vision, as Krishnan has also suggested, is without a shred of evidence.

Views of vision specialists

At the suggestion of our own ophthalmological consultant for this study, Dr. Perry Seamonds, we prepared a brief technical report of our preliminary findings and sent it to several leading American vision specialists he recommended as well as to a couple of others who we thought might be interested in our work. In our covering letter we invited them to offer their own views concerning possible interpretations of our findings or to suggest any possible artifacts or methodological shortcomings that might need to be taken into account in any assessment of our work.

None of the four persons who replied was able to offer any conventional explanation for our results based on their own field of expertise, which was also the response of our own consultant, Dr. Seamonds. In general, their comments focused on the difficulties of defining blindness, being sure that those who were classified as blind from birth were truly always and completely without sight, and wondering about the wisdom of including adventitiously blind and severely visually impaired persons in our study. One suggested that perhaps some of our blind from birth respondents may have been describing what they had already learned through touch or verbal contact. No one, in our opinion, made any serious attempt to grapple with our findings or the problems they appear to raise for conventional science. One of our correspondents did concede, however, "If a blind person from infancy can describe in detail a complex object or scene during an NDE, then I think you are really onto something."

An assessment of the evidence for alternative explanations

At the beginning of this chapter, we raised the question, "Might there not be non-retinal-based mechanisms that could in principle account for the results of this study and thus demonstrate that vision in the blind is indeed only apparent and not actual?" In searching for such an explanation, we have considered theories and data relating to dreams, retrospective reconstruction, blindsight and skin-based vision, in addition to the views of a few selected vision specialists—and have come up empty. Of course, it would be absurd to claim that we have exhausted the list of naturalistic or conventional possibilities here or eliminated all conceivable artifacts, but we believe we have

ruled out some of the most obvious candidates for
explanatory honors. At the very least, we have perhaps
managed to cast some doubt on the tenability of this *type* of
explanation for our findings, and consequently increased
the likelihood that however they might be accounted for,
we would do best to seek elsewhere for our answers.

In any case, having addressed this basic issue, we
can now revert to the question we posed earlier about
whether or in what sense it can be said that the blind do see.
Clearly before *any* explanation for vision in the blind can
be accepted, it must first be established that their reports
reflect the operation of something that can legitimately be
called "true sight." That assumption has of course been
implicit throughout most of this book and may perhaps
appear to some to be self-evident by now. But it is not, and
our next task is to demonstrate just why.

Apparent vision in the blind: Is it really seeing?

In Chapter Four, we presented the case of an
adventitiously blind woman named Marilyn who, it will be
recalled, had a great deal of difficulty in deciding whether
she could truly affirm that she had a visual impression of
her body during her NDE. In the end, she appeared to be
comfortable with the statement that she had had a kind of
"semi-visual" experience, but its exact nature remained
elusive and her interview as a whole raised some
perplexing questions about the tenability of a literal
interpretation of the claims that the blind sometimes appear
to make that they did indeed see during their NDEs or
OBEs. The momentary doubts that Marilyn's testimony
evoked will now have to be dealt with more fully, for it is
finally time to begin to probe beneath the *surface*
descriptions of these experiences in order to get a feel for

their underlying texture and quality before they are slipped into the convenient clothes of ordinary language. And in this connection, it is important, we think, to remind the reader of an obvious, but easily overlooked, point: In undertaking this analysis, we must be especially mindful that of course we can never have access to anything like the pure NDE or OBE in itself. Every such experience is coded in a certain way as it occurs, and after it occurs, and comes to us only later as a report in a linguistic form. Therefore, by the time we interview our respondents, the original experience has already been processed through several distinct filters, necessarily undergoing a series of virtually unconscious transformations until it reaches us as a distinct and coherent narrative.

What we need to do here, however, is to see if we can begin to learn at least something about the way this narrative comes to be shaped, and how the experience may have been coded in the first place. For this purpose, we will be drawing on the interviews of several selected respondents, two of them previously unmentioned, as well as segments from other interviews where these matters were also explored in some depth.

One of these respondents was a forty-year-old woman named Claudia who as a child never saw well and lost her sight completely by the age of five. When she was thirty-six, she was raped and during that attack had an OBE in which she saw her physical body from above. Or did she? Let us look closely at her own testimony on this issue, which she discussed at several points in her interview. At the beginning, for example, she was asked:

Interviewer: What did you notice when you were looking down? Did you see your body?
Claudia: Yeah, I did.

Interviewer: You did. Was that the first time you remember seeing your body, I mean visually?

Claudia: It wasn't visual. It's really hard to describe because it wasn't visual. It was almost like a tactile thing, except that there was no way I could have touched from up there. But it really wasn't visual because I just don't have vision any more.... It [was] sort of like a tactile memory or something. It's not really like vision is. Vision is more clear, but it's also more tied down.

And, later, she recalls something else about the room in which she was raped that makes it seem impossible that what she was aware of could have been a simple visual impression. She believes she was assaulted on the lower of two bunk beds, the top one of which should have obscured her vision of herself down below from where she found herself observing. But as she pointed out to us:

> The other thing that's weird is, if I remember right, yeah, it was a bunk bed so I couldn't have seen from the ceiling. So it wasn't like vision is.

Toward the end of the interview, we asked Claudia to try to elaborate on her sense of this aspect of her experience for us and to tease it apart. Here, the interviewer prefaces her first question with a summary of what Claudia had told us thus far:

Interviewer: If you wouldn't mind, I would like to ask a couple of questions in terms of visual perception. I know we've talked about visual perception and I know you've said that that's a hard concept to describe. For instance, you saw yourself on the bed—and I know you said it wasn't quite like sight but then again it wasn't that you were touching the person. The bunk bed didn't block your view. Did you feel you had, on some level, visual perception of yourself even though it wasn't how you would see through the eyes?

Claudia: I guess if you want to call it visual. I just kind of hesitate to call it visual because of the little I remember what vision was like. But as far as it being a perception that's kind of like a visual perception, I would have to say yes. But it wasn't exactly the same as that. I didn't suddenly see. I didn't see at all. But I was aware of things in a way that was kind of tactile ... even though from where I was I couldn't have had any tactile experience of it and that's the difference....

Interviewer: It sounds like you're not quite sure what category to put it in.

Claudia: Yeah, I'm not. It's kind of like vision but it's not vision.... It was seeing but it wasn't vision... because vision is really sharp and it wasn't like that.

Interviewer: But you said it was clear.

Claudia: Yeah, it's clear in the sense that it's there and all the details are there. But what I remember of seeing [is that] things are more, they are kind of more detailed. This [experience] didn't have that kind of detail.

Clearly, there are distinct echoes here of Marilyn's earlier testimony: There is a kind of seeing without vision. It is hard to know exactly how to understand the distinction, but to us it appears that what at least some of these respondents are suggesting is that it is more like a general apprehension of the situation rather than merely a clear and detailed *picture* of it. It is almost as if one somehow *knows* what is happening without actually perceiving it in a way that conforms to their understanding of ordinary sight. Finally, it is of interest to note Claudia's feeling that there was, despite its seeming impossibility, something *tactile* about her perception, too, as though that was an aspect of her coding process. We will see that this tactile sense is actually not infrequently mentioned by other blind respondents as a part of the felt texture of their experiences.

Another of our respondents whose testimony was extremely helpful in giving us a fix on these issues was Harold, a forty-one-year-old man who had lost his sight completely as a result of an automobile accident when he was sixteen. In the emergency room of a hospital following the accident, he had an NDE during which he had an undeniable sense of separating from his body and a perception of himself down below where a medical team was working on him. But exactly what that perception was like and how it could best be characterized are the questions we must closely examine next. For this purpose, we will again present a brief extract from his interview, a portion of which has already been cited in connection with our consideration of the alternative hypothesis of retrospective reconstruction. Before presenting his testimony, we should make it clear that Harold insists that he was immediately blinded in the accident and at no time thereafter, including when he was in the emergency room, did he have any physical vision whatever.

Harold: It was during that emergency, the activity in the room, that I just felt like I was observing everything. And it wasn't a vivid observation.... I was more aware of being apart from the whole scene than I was aware of seeing visual detail and specific stuff.... But I felt like I was watching the whole thing.... What I saw was less realistic than dream-like. There was no vividness or sense of detail whatsoever. I can't say that I saw the doctor's fingers do this or saw the look on his face, you know.

Interviewer: But you did see the forms themselves working on you?

Harold: I was aware of them. I didn't perceive them in a visual sense.

Interviewer: You did not?

Harold: Yeah, 'cause I hadn't even really adapted to being blind, so I think what it was that was happening here was a bunch of synesthesia, where all these perceptions were being blended into some image in my mind, you know, the visual, the tactile, all the input that I had. I can't literally say I really saw anything, but yet I was aware of what was going on, and perceiving all that in my mind.... But I don't remember detail. That's why I say I'm loath to describe it as a visual. I mean, I'd like to make it as dramatic as possible, but I'm not gonna add anything beyond what I think is literally the facts.... I feel more comfortable with the word "perceive" rather than "see" because.... I don't know whether I was just visualizing it ... rather than literally seeing it.

Here again, we mark the respondent's unwillingness to frame his experience in purely visual terms despite the temptation to make his testimony "as dramatic as possible." But, like Claudia, he insists that to do so would be to distort, not to describe, his experience. In his case, however, he appears to make a distinction between *visualizing* his experience (i.e., creating a purely mental representation of it) and seeing it, as if he was able to put it together from a combination of cues available in his environment and thereby form a coherent, if non-specific, image of his situation in his mind. Once more, there seems to be an implication that the resultant representation is more a mix of various perceptual and cognitive factors rather than anything resembling an analog to the sensation of physically-mediated sight itself.

This interpretation is suggested not only by the comments of respondents we have previously not had an occasion to introduce, but is also supported by some of the statements subsequently made by Brad, for instance, whose earlier testimony seemed to reflect unambiguous evidence for a more literal understanding of apparent vision in the blind. In a second interview with him on July 23, 1995, we learned some things that caused us to want to qualify somewhat the conclusions seemingly implied by his original narrative. Specifically, in recalling his memory of the scene of the snow on the streets outside his school, he now told us:

> I was quite aware of all the things that were physically mentioned in there [i.e., his earlier description]. However, whether it was seen visually through the eyes, I could not say.... I mean, you have to remember, being born blind, I had no idea whether these images were visual.... It was something like a tactual sense, like I could literally feel with the fingers of my mind. But I did not remember actually touching the snow.... The only thing I can really state about those images was that they came to me in an awareness and that I was aware of those images in a way I did not really understand. I could not really say that they were visual *per se* because I had never known anything like that before. But I could say that all my senses seemed to be very active and very much aware. I was aware. I had a clear sense of touch and smell and even taste.

Brad, too, seems to be telling us now that he cannot be certain his representation of the snow was in any definitive sense "visual" *per se,* especially since he has no real understanding of what a visual image is. Instead, as with Harold, a complex multi-sensory awareness seems to have been involved, and, in a remarkable similarity with Claudia, Brad makes an almost identical statement to hers about the tactile quality of his impression, again suggesting that this modality may be a key feature in the coding of these experiences by the blind, as it certainly is in their daily life.

Even Vicki, in subsequent exchanges with us, eventually clarified her previous statements concerning whether her experiences could be properly thought of as examples of pure seeing. In our interview with her on May 27, 1994, for instance, she allowed, "It was scary at first.... I had trouble relating things to one another, what I was seeing and perceiving versus what I had touched and known the way I had known things all my life." And in a phone conversation the following year, on July 18, 1995, when one of us (K.R.) asked her whether in her opinion it was a matter of seeing or knowing in her experience, she unhesitatingly replied, "It's both, Ken, it's both seeing and knowing."

And still other respondents have made similar utterances to us. One of those who had an OBE, upon viewing her body down below, wondered, "How do you describe it? You know, you just know. And I don't know if you could say it was actually seeing, but you knew." Another OBEr averred, "What I'm saying is I was more aware. I don't know if it's through sight that I was aware.... I'm not sure. All I know is ... somehow I was aware of information or things that were going on that I wouldn't normally be able to pick up through seeing.... That's why I'm being very careful how I'm wording it, 'cause I'm not sure where it came from. I would say to you I have a feeling it didn't come from seeing, and yet I'm not sure."

As this kind of testimony builds, it seems more and more difficult to claim that the blind simply *see* (in the strict sense of visual perception) what they report. Rather, it is beginning to appear it is more a matter of their *knowing*, through a still poorly understood mode of generalized awareness based on a variety of sensory impressions, including tactile ones, what is happening around them. The question that immediately confronts us now, however, is as unavoidable as it is crucial: *Why is it, then, that these reports, when casually perused, nevertheless often seem to imply that the blind* do *see in a way akin to physical sight?*

By this point, the answer, we believe, should be fairly obvious. However these experiences may have been coded originally, by the time we encounter them they have long come to be expressed in a particular linguistic form. And that form is a *language of vision*, since our ordinary language is rooted in the experiences of sighted persons and is therefore biased in favor of *visual* imagery, concepts and words. Because the blind are members of the same linguistic community as sighted persons, we can certainly expect that they will tend—indeed will be virtually compelled—to phrase their experiences in a language of vision, almost regardless of its appropriateness to the qualities of their own personal experience.

And this is not just speculation on our part—other researchers have reported findings in support of the same conclusions (e.g. Cook, 1970, Rathna, 1962). We have plenty of evidence of precisely this sort of thing from our own respondents, too, whose tendency to fall into a language of vision—even when it is patently at variance with the nature of their perception—is so habitual as to be mostly unconscious. To take just a casual instance, whose significance then was not immediately apparent to us, we remember being struck by Vicki's saying that she likes to "watch" television, or by her injunctions to a friend, "to look at this."

And even when blind persons are aware of the incongruity of their language, they may still resort to it out of a short-term expediency. Said one of our respondents in this connection: "Most people who have been blind for a long time don't have a problem with saying, 'I saw Jay Leno last night on TV' when they don't mean that they actually physically saw the man, but that they 'watched' his show. People get hung up on that and that's no problem for me."

Perhaps the most unabashed statement along these lines came to us in a letter from one of our respondents, whom we will call Candy, after she attended a lecture in which the preliminary findings from our research project were shared in full for the first time. In commenting on our hypothesis, Candy wrote:

> You mentioned in your presentation how some blind people use vision words in their vocabulary. I wanted to share my thoughts with you regarding such visual references perhaps to help you know why. I once belonged to a national organization for blind people and attended annual conventions full of blind people. I say this only to say that almost every blind person that I have ever met does indeed use such visual language. I can tell you that they don't mean it literally; instead they use such terms quite figuratively. Very simply, the reason why blind people say things such as, "I watch TV," or "I saw your keys on the table," and the like, is because we live in a sighted world.

> If you are around any certain type of language long enough, like it or not or however awkward it may seem, you eventually start to use it.... Professors often use the term, "if you will." A few times that expression started to come out of my mouth until I stopped dead in my tracks. I had been exposed to it

for so long it almost naturally wanted to become a part of my language. So it is with visual phrases such as, "have you seen the cat?" If everyone you know and everywhere you go visual terminology is used it seems downright awkward not to. For example, wouldn't it sound ridiculous to say, "I just felt the cat in the kitchen," as opposed to "I just saw the cat in the kitchen."

Brad, in the same interview from which we just quoted, likewise voiced statements identical to Candy's about the social pressures on the blind to use a common language of vision. Speaking of his own tendencies in this respect, he told us:

What I would often do when I describe things or notice certain things was I would use the word, "see," to actually mean "hear" or "touch" or "smell" or some other thing. And I might use the word, "see," just as I notice other people around me would use the word, "see" or "watch," or any sort of sight word whatsoever. So I tended to amalgamate my vocabulary with anyone else's.... What it was for me was a compensatory way of basically allowing myself to fit in with the rest of society in using the same language, *although meaning something else completely* (italics ours).

What such comments as these imply insofar as our own reports are concerned is that we must now be alert not just to the possibility but to the *likelihood* that the blind tend to use vision verbs in ways both looser than and different from that of sighted persons. In short, in ordinary conversation when a blind person says he or she *sees* something, we should not necessarily infer that what is meant conforms to common usage. This is especially true, of course, for those persons who have not ever had any experience with sight, as Candy made clear in another passage in her letter:

> When someone who was blind at birth attempts to visually describe something to you as they, so-called, "saw" it, that might mean something entirely different from someone such as myself who had sight for twenty-one years.

In summary, what we have learned in this section from our respondents is that although their experiences may sometimes be *expressed* in a language of vision, a close reading of their transcripts suggests something closer to a multifaceted synesthetic perception that seems to involve much more than an analog of physical sight. Now, this is not to say that as part of this awareness there cannot be some sort of pictorial imagery as well; it is only to assert that this must not be taken in any simplistic way as constituting vision as we normally understand it.

Eyeless vision and transcendental awareness

Even if we cannot assert that the blind *see* in these experiences in any straightforward way, we still have to reckon with the fact—and it does seem to be a fact—that they nevertheless do have access to a kind of expanded supersensory awareness that may in itself not be explicable by normal means. Furthermore, notwithstanding the cases of indistinct and nebulous "sight" we have just reviewed, we must not overlook the ineluctable and very unequivocal claims on the part of most of our respondents that they did seem to possess a type of vision that was very keen, detailed and even "crystal clear" at times. Perhaps, as we have suggested, even if these reports may not in the end represent an analog of retinal vision as such, they clearly represent *something* that must be directly addressed. Thus, it remains for us to grapple with this question "Well, if it isn't *seeing*, what in blazes *is* it?"

To pursue this line of inquiry, the first point we must note is that obviously the blind simply represent a kind of limit case in research dealing with alleged perceptions while in a near-death or out-of-body state. If blind persons report what they cannot possibly see—since they have no physically-mediated sight—or what they cannot know by other normal means, as seems to be so in at least some instances in our study, then we have clearly identified a phenomenon that threatens to cast a dark shadow on the house of conventional science. But it is equally plain that *whenever* we can show that such perceptions are physically impossible, whether with blind persons or not, the same kind of shadow appears—as indeed it already has, many times, in other research dealing with NDEs and OBEs. So to begin to focus more clearly on precisely what it is we need to explain here, let us look for a moment at a few illustrative cases one step removed from those we have considered in this report where "impossible perceptions" of great acuity are described by the poorly sighted.

One type of case that has long intrigued us, for example, is when such individuals are seemingly able to report such fine and improbably noticed features as, say, "dust on the light fixtures" in an operating room when, from the location of their physical body at the time as well as their eyesight, such perceptions would manifestly be impossible. Here, then, are a couple of such instances from our previous research.

One of them comes from a woman interviewed in the early 1980s who was forty-eight years old at the time

(Ring, 1984). She had had her NDE in connection with a surgical procedure in 1974. What was especially noteworthy about her account at the outset, however, was her mention of her unusually garbed anesthesiologist. As she explained, he was a physician who often worked with children. And because he had found that his young patients often were confused by a team of similarly clad green-garmented doctors, he had taken to wearing a yellow surgical hat with magenta butterflies on it so he, at least, could easily be recognized. All this will, of course, be highly relevant to this woman's account of her experience which will now be described in her own words. She had gone into shock when she heard her physician exclaim, "This woman's dying!" At that point:

> Bang, I left! The next thing I was aware of was floating on the ceiling. And seeing down there, with his hat on his head, I knew who he was because of the hat on his head [i.e., the anesthesiologist with the magenta butterfly cap] ... it was so vivid. I'm very nearsighted, too, by the way, which was another one of the startling things that happened to me when I left my body. I see at fifteen feet what most people see at four hundred.... They were hooking me up to a machine that was behind my head. And my very first thought was, "Jesus, I can see! I can't believe it, I can see!" I could read the numbers on the machine behind my head and I was just so thrilled. And I thought, "They gave me back my glasses...." (Ring, 1984, p. 42)

She goes on to describe further details of her operation, including how her body looked, the shaving of her belly, and various medical procedures that her surgical team were performing upon her, and then finds herself looking at another object from a position high above her physical body:

> From where I was looking, I could look down on this enormous fluorescent light ... and it was so dirty on top of the light. [Could you see the top of the light fixture?] Yes, and it was filthy. And I remember thinking, "Got to tell the nurses about that" (Ring, 1984, p. 43).

One of the striking features of this case, of course, is this woman's observation that she was able to see so clearly during her NDE despite the fact that, as she avers, she is very nearsighted. In this respect, too, this woman's testimony is far from unique in our records. Another very similar story is told, for example, in a letter from an audiologist who likewise reports seeing dust on the light fixtures of the operating room where his NDE took place. This incident occurred in a Japanese hospital during the Korean War. In addition, this same man, who became interested in NDEs as a result of his own experience, also learned of another case, involving a nurse at the same hospital, which had a remarkable correspondence to his. On this point, as he states in his letter:

> The odd thing about both of our experiences is that we are both extremely myopic, i.e., thick glasses and blind as bats six inches from our noses. And yet we were both able to describe accurately events, dials, details, expressions in our OBEs, without our glasses.

Such highly acute visual perceptions on the part of the poorly sighted are hardly limited to those who are apparently hovering above their bodies during NDEs. Other non-ordinary states of consciousness, such as meditation, can also sometimes evoke them. Here is a particularly compelling example from a book by a well-known optometrist whose uncorrected eyesight was 20/200:

> [At this time] I was meditating every day.... During one of these deep meditative states, I had a very profound and startling experience. Although my eyes were closed, I could suddenly see everything—the whole room and myself in it—and I couldn't tell where I was seeing from! I wasn't seeing from my eyes or from any single point of view. I seemed to be seeing everything from everywhere. There seemed to be eyes in every cell of my body and in every particle surrounding me. I could simultaneously see from straight on, from above, from below, from behind, and so on.... There seemed to be no observer separate from what was seen. There was simply awareness (Liberman, 1995, p. 47).

Here we have an important clue about the nature of this kind of "seeing." It may not be limited to the kind of concentrated focus we sometimes encounter in cases of NDEs, where one's perceptual attention sometimes seems restricted to the physical body. Instead, as this account shows, one's awareness can be *omnidirectional.* In fact, this type of perception *is* sometimes reported by those having NDEs or OBEs, and it is precisely this feature that suggests that "awareness" is a more appropriate term for this experience than is "seeing," as the writer just quoted also implies. In this new context, then, consider this account from an NDEr whose experience occurred as a result of pneumonia during her second pregnancy. During this crisis, the woman was rushed to the hospital by her husband and, upon arrival, lost consciousness. Still, she was able to hear the nurses talking about her, saying that she was "dead meat." Nevertheless, she herself was elsewhere at the time. As she relates her experience:

> I was hovering over a stretcher in one of the emergency rooms at the hospital. I glanced down at the stretcher, knew the body wrapped in blankets was mine, and really didn't care. The room was much more interesting than my body. And what a neat perspective. I could see everything. And I do mean everything! I could see the top of the light on the ceiling and the underside of the stretcher. I could see the tiles on the ceiling and the tiles on the floor, simultaneously. Three hundred sixty degree spherical vision. And not just spherical. Detailed! I could see every single hair and the follicle out of which it grew on the head of the nurse standing beside the stretcher. At the time I knew exactly how many hairs there were to look at. But I shifted focus. She was wearing glittery white nylons. Every single shimmer and sheen stood out in glowing detail, and once again I knew exactly how many sparkles there were.

In this narrative, we notice again not only this astonishing feature of omnidirectional awareness, but also a type of knowledge that, if this NDEr is not engaging in hyperbole (though other NDErs we have interviewed have spoken in precisely the same terms), stretches our concept of ordinary "vision" beyond the breaking point. Clearly, this is not simple "vision" at all as we are wont to understand it, but almost a kind of seeming omniscience that completely transcends what mere seeing could ever afford. Indeed, what we appear to have here is a distinctive state of consciousness, which we would like to call *transcendental awareness*, or *mindsight*. In this type of awareness, it is not, of course, that the eyes see anything—how could they? It is rather that the *mind itself* sees, but more in the sense of "understanding" or "taking in" than of visual perception *per se*. Or alternatively, we might say that it is not the eye that sees, but the "I."

Celia Green (1968) an English psychologist who some years ago conducted an important survey of OBEs, found evidence for much the same concept as we are calling mindsight, among her respondents, too. Just to cite one brief relevant instance here, she quotes one of her subjects as saying, "having no eyes, I 'saw' with whole consciousness" (p. 70).

And indeed her survey is chock-full of cases showing many of the very same features we have found in our study of the blind. Thus we have instances of keenly detailed perceptions, which some of her subjects, like ours, characterize as "crystal clear," or say things like, "I could see the room in great detail, even the specks of dust" (Green, 1968, p. 72). Green also reports examples of apparent sight through physical obstacles (p. 83) and multi-sensory or synesthetic experiences (p. 70). Therefore, what students of OBEs tend to call *extrasomatic vision* seems to be identical to what we prefer to call, for reasons we now explain, transcendental awareness or mindsight.

Our partiality to this particular terminology hinges on our previous discussion about the ubiquity of a language of vision. In effect, we wish to argue that the blind, like other persons reporting OBEs (29) and NDEs, have entered into a state of transcendental awareness—which confers an access to a realm of knowledge not available in one's normal waking state—but then are forced, again just like others, to translate their experiences into visual metaphors. Thus, the supersensory kind of *knowing* that the experience provides becomes *seeing* when it undergoes the necessity of linguistic transformation. That's why NDErs and OBErs, including some of our blind respondents, speak *as if* they have seen, but that, we conclude, is an almost unavoidable distortion required by common language usage.

Thus, in answer to our earlier question, "Well, if it isn't seeing, what in blazes *is* it?," we submit that it is transcendental awareness, a distinctive state of consciousness and mode of knowing in its own right, which is operative in the blind *and* sighted persons alike during their experiences and which now stands in need of explanation. But at least we have, we believe, finally identified the phenomenon itself that seems to underlie and make possible the claims that the blind can "see" during their NDEs and OBEs, and why it is that their apparent "vision" can sometimes be so extraordinarily detailed and fine as to be, in their mind, "perfect." (30) Since mindsight, by implication, must transcend the limitations of the senses, it is possible, at least at times, for one to have access to a state of consciousness where, with "the doors of perception cleansed," everything presents itself in true Blakean fashion, "as it is, infinite."

Some readers, especially those of a parapsychological bent, may wonder why we have elected to use the expression, transcendental awareness, when we might perhaps have resorted to an already familiar term, viz., clairvoyant vision, a type of extrasensory perception. (31) To some degree, this is a matter of personal preference, but it is not, we think, a wholly arbitrary choice. To us, the term clairvoyant vision implies something closer to a type of perception that is not mediated by the senses, whereas what we are keen to emphasize is the *epistemic* nature of an experience that is disclosed by accessing a distinctive mode of awareness. As we conceive it, this is more a realm of knowledge than a type of perception as such. Certainly, when one thinks about the transcendental visions and the influx of universal knowledge during the otherworldly portions of an NDE, this point becomes almost apodictic in its obviousness. At the same time, there is evidence, which we will shortly review, that there is decidedly a relationship between clairvoyant vision and what we have called mindsight. In our view, the latter subsumes the former and is therefore the more inclusive concept. To begin to explore this relationship, however, we need to return to our explication of the concept of transcendental awareness itself.

Before we close in on this concept, then, and try to understand how the operation of this type of consciousness could, in principle, afford the kind of "impossible knowledge" the blind gain during their experiences, we need to recall one further clue about its nature. This has to do with various hints that have scattered themselves along the trail of our inquiry that there may be, after all, a certain multi-sensory or synesthetic quality to transcendental awareness.

Remember, for example, that Harold made explicit reference to a synesthetic quality in his NDE, and likewise Brad mentioned that his seemed to involve a kind of multi-sensory awareness. Other respondents indicated to us that they, too, find themselves experiencing synesthesias, even in their everyday experience. For example, Carla told us, "I wonder if I'm bordering on synesthesia or something, because different colors have different sounds for me.... I always *hear* color. It's so natural for me.... It's like people see words. I hear color." And then we have all those cases—and we did not bother to cite them all previously—where respondents talk about a kind of compounding or conflation of visual and tactile modes of awareness. Furthermore, it is not implausible to suppose that other respondents *might* have mentioned synesthetic elements in their experiences, had they been familiar with the concept.

The possible implication of synesthesia in NDEs and OBEs is a hypothesis that is far from original with us. Phyllis Atwater (1988) for example, several years ago, tried to draw researchers' attention to this possibility, while H. J. Irwin (1985, 1987) and Celia Green (1968) have already done so for the study of OBEs. Green, for example, quotes one of her subjects as explicitly claiming his OBE-based perception was a form of synesthesia, "saying that it involved no one sensory modality but was 'comprehensive.'" (p. 70).

And the concept of synesthesia may be relevant not only to NDEs and OBEs but to various forms of ESP as well. Just to give one little but intriguing illustration to support this possibility, consider the work of Yoichiro Sako and Shuji Homma (1997). In one study they investigated the clairvoyant abilities of seven school children. Here, they used as targets hidden drawings of objects that are normally associated with various sensory modalities (e.g, a drawing of a cake, a running faucet, a phone, etc.). A number of the children were not only uncannily accurate in their drawings of these objects, but in describing how they came to depict what they did, they sometimes mentioned clear-cut synthesthetic processes. For example, one student whose concealed target was a drawing of a wind chime said that he first *heard* the sounds, "ring, ring," then *felt* something "wavering by the wind," and finally received a mental image of the chime. Another child, given a lit cigarette as a target, reported at first a "dim vision" of something like a pipe, followed immediately by a strange and nasty smell, like something burning. Swiftly, a sense of smoke suggested to her that it was a burning cigarette.

Our suggestion, which builds on these speculations and research findings, merely goes one step further in postulating that such synesthesias might be conceptualized as forming an aspect of transcendental awareness itself. And, along these lines, it might be worth noting that if one delves into the esoteric literature, which is obviously rooted in axiomatic assumptions having to do with transcendental awareness, one can also find intriguing references to a synesthetically-informed consciousness in near-death states. For example, in Yogananda's classic work, *Autobiography of a Yogi* (1946/1972), the claim is made that while in the "astral" state, knowledge bypasses the "outer sensory organs" and is filtered through a direct intuitional sense instead. When this occurs, individuals, we are told, "can see through the ear or nose or skin. They are able to hear through the eyes or tongue, and can taste through the ears or skin, and so forth" (p. 481).

Whatever one makes of this last apparent convergence from the esoteric literature, the fact remains that, as we have seen, there are already sufficient clues pointing to a possible role for synesthetic processing in states of transcendental awareness so that any proposed explanation for this type of consciousness must be prepared to take them into account. Furthermore, the connection we have already alluded to between synesthesias and clairvoyance suggests to us that a full explication of the concept of transcendental awareness must somehow also incorporate clairvoyant vision as an integral component of this type of awareness.

Thus, we end by positing that a complex form of synesthetically modulated awareness with clairvoyant aspects is ultimately responsible for the results reported in this study. Just *how* this kind of consciousness—transcendental awareness—might function to afford access to such conventionally inexplicable knowledge is the last station on our explanatory journey, and we arrive there next.

Theories of transcendental awareness

When confronted with the evidence for transcendental awareness we have presented in this book—both from our own study of the blind as well as the research findings of others—it is tempting, in searching for an explanatory framework to encompass such anomalous data, to resort to the esoteric traditions that appear so ready to accommodate what conventional science cannot. Insofar as our specific findings are concerned, the ancient notion of subtle bodies, for example, is an obvious and relevant candidate for an appealing explanatory concept here. This construct, which, as J.J. Poortman (1978) has shown, stems from some of the earliest spiritual texts of India and Egypt, persisted through the Old Testament and ancient Greek and Neoplatonic philosophy, and ultimately found perhaps its most recent apogee in the theories of such modern esotericists as Helena Blavatsky and Rudolf Steiner. In essence, it postulates the existence of several bodies, or vehicles, beyond the physical, which together constitute our true nature.

In most formulations of this kind, it is said that in addition to the physical (or gross) body, we have a so-called etheric body (or "sheath"), an astral body, a mental body, a causal body, and so forth, with each successive body becoming more subtle and refined, and vibrating at higher levels, all of them, however, being intertwined with and interpenetrating one another. Although, of course, we are normally aware only of our physical being, these other bodies, especially the etheric and astral, are held to have some properties that represent, as it were, higher-level expressions of the components of the physical system to which they correspond. Among them is the subtle body equivalent of *the eye* which, when it is activated, is believed to afford something that one could call, we suppose, a kind of "astral vision."

If one were to invoke this sort of approach to explain our findings, here is how it would work, according to one modern thinker (Steinpach, 1980) who directed himself to precisely the question our research brings to the fore. He is discussing at this point the awareness of out-of-body perception in the context of an unfolding NDE:

> The next perplexingly new experience then is that of the "out-of-body state," of no-longer-being-in-the-body. Here the soul, no longer held fast enough by the body-radiation, has already drawn the astral body off the physical body, and the real man, the spirit, now looks through this astral body at the physical body. In this state the persons were able to see what was happening around this physical body.... But how is this possible?

> Here too, it is a matter of something completely natural. Just as in the gross material eyes and the gross material organs of hearing our gross material body possesses sense-organs corresponding to its consistency, so also the astral body and the ethereal body have the particular homogeneous [sic] equipment corresponding to them. But it is always our spirit which sees, hears or feels through the sense-organs of the particular outermost covering, thus never the eye or the ear itself. The spirit within the astral body thus perceives through the sense-organs of the latter. (Steinpach, 1980, p. 28)

According to this formulation, then, the blind can see because, with the physical body temporarily inoperative, the spirit within them can make use of the finer sense organs of the astral body, which presumably are perfect, to gain temporarily a kind of vision they could never have in life.

Of course, this is possible, but from a scientific point of view, this type of thinking is not useful as an explanatory vehicle. It is obvious, for instance, that it rests on various *ad hoc* assumptions and concepts that make it immune from any testable (or falsifiable) consequences. This is not meant to impugn the teachings of great occultists, such as Rudolf Steiner, who from all evidence did have the kind of "super-sensible clairvoyant sight" (Roszell, 1992, Steiner, 1989; Wilson, 1987) that permitted him to assert with confidence that this multi-bodied view of the human being was indeed correct. But esoteric truth is one thing, and scientific truth another, and there are very different canons of acceptance for each. In our view, it is better not to mix these up and preferable, whenever possible, to search for an interpretative perspective that itself accords with the basic criteria that modern science insists upon for its explanatory models.

And we believe that such a perspective now exists, although, to be sure, it is not to be found in today's conventional science. If we turn instead, however, to some recent developments in New Paradigm science, we can quickly discern the shape of the explanation we need to seek.

In recent years, a number of thinkers, influenced by developments in modern physics, have elaborated a variety of theories of consciousness which, despite their somewhat different basic postulates, *all* either predict or imply that blind persons should be able to have something like visual perception during NDEs and OBEs. In addition, all of these theories explicitly address the phenomenon of the NDE in general and also posit the existence of a state of consciousness that corresponds to what we have called here mindsight. Among such formulations that will be of special interest to us are Kenneth Arnette's "Theory of Essence" (1992, 1995a, 1995b, 1995c), Larry's Dossey's "Nonlocality Theory of Consciousness" (1989), Amit Goswami's "Quantum Theory of Consciousness" (1993, 1994, 1995a, 1995b), Michael Talbot's "Holographic Theory of Consciousness" (1991), and Jenny Wade's "Holonomic Theory of Consciousness" (1996a, 1996b).

As indicated, the ground philosophic assumptions of these theories vary. For instance, Arnette's position is one of explicit dualistic interactionism, Goswami's, a monistic idealism which nevertheless is able to incorporate some of the insights of dualistic theories without having to resort to dualism *per se,* while Wade's approach represents an uncompromising nondualism. Nevertheless, these theorists all agree about certain properties of consciousness itself, and on this basis they can serve as a kind of collective expression of the point of view we believe best articulates our own theoretical convictions. Let's examine next, then, this list of the common postulates of these theories having to do with the nature of consciousness.

First, *consciousness itself is primary and is the ground of all being.* Goswami's (1994) statements here are indicative of this position and sum it up succinctly: "...all events are phenomena in consciousness. Beyond what we see as immanent reality, there is a transcendent reality; ultimately all reality is comprised of consciousness. The division of reality into transcendental and immanent is an epiphenomenon of experience" (p.1).

Second, *consciousness is nonlocal.* What this assertion implies is that Mind, rather than being located in the individual and bounded by time (i.e., birth and death), is fixed neither in time nor space. In fact, in this view, it is not really appropriate, except as a shorthand convenience, to speak of the mind; instead there is, as our first proposition implies, only Mind. This insight, though derivative from a nonlocality position, may be stated as a separate assumption, as follows:

Third, *consciousness is unitive.* That is, there is only one consciousness, which we call Mind, and the notion of individual minds is at bottom nothing more than a useful fiction that Dossey (1989) pointedly calls "the illusion of a separate self and the sensation of an ego that possesses a separate mind" (p. 98).

Fourth, *consciousness may and indeed must sometimes function independently of the brain.* This is a key assumption, especially for understanding how the blind may become aware of something that seems like visual perception, so we will need to linger a bit over it in order to tease out its implications of special relevance to us. Dossey (1989) again states the matter with admirable concision: "... if the mind is nonlocal, it must in some sense be independent of the strictly local brain and body.... And if the mind is nonlocal, unconfined to brains and bodies and thus not entirely dependent on the physical organism, the possibility of survival of bodily death is opened" (p. 7). Of course, as Dossey elsewhere points out and as all of the other theorists under consideration here would agree, although Mind is neither confined to the brain nor a product of it, of course it may work *through the brain* to give us our representation of the phenomenal world. According to Goswami (1995a) our ordinary perception of time and space comes about as a result of a quantum-mechanical process whereby consciousness self-referentially "collapses" what are called "probability waves" so as to give rise to actuality: "In the process of collapse, one undivided consciousness sees itself as *apparently* divided into dualities such as life and environment, subject and object" (p. 5).

Thus, what we have here is an adumbration of a process that begins with Mind, fully independent of brain, becoming self-referential (that is, becoming *identified* with consciousness itself), and then *converting* this noumenal consciousness into a dualistic modality that generates the familiar phenomenal world.

What we have called mindsight is at least the beginning of the *reversal* of that process by which, even though the traces of an everyday dualism remain, the individual is enabled, however temporarily, to experience the world from a perspective independent of brain functioning and the operation of the senses. That each of these theories formally entails such a state of awareness, *specifically* in blind persons during NDEs or OBEs, we shall now demonstrate, and in doing so, attempt to translate their hitherto abstract propositions into a discourse that speaks directly to the data from this study.

How theorists of transcendental awareness address the possibility of "seeing" in the blind

As we did in the case of our vision specialists, whenever possible we solicited the views of these New Paradigm theorists concerning our findings, and in what follows we shall, in some cases, be quoting from special commentaries they prepared for us for this purpose. We offer the perspective of these theorists in the hope that their formulations will afford the basis for deriving important testable implications concerning transcendental awareness and other states of non-ordinary consciousness.

Taking these theorists now in the same (alphabetical) order in which they were presented originally, we may begin with some pertinent remarks by Kenneth Arnette, the author of what he calls "A Theory of Essence." We can't of course take the time here to expound each of these theories as such, so suffice it to say that Arnette postulates that human beings are comprised of a material body and a non-physical component, which he calls "essence." Essence is "our consciousness, our awareness, our individual personality, and it survives the death of the body" (Arnette, 1995c, p. 1). Although the body/brain unit and essence are radically different, Arnette believes they do interact with each other through their separately generated electromagnetic fields. Arnette argues that his theory actually would *predict* a kind of vision in the blind during NDEs. As he put it to us:

> In addition to interacting with the body, the essence can, when dissociated from the body, interact with electromagnetic radiation (light) to give a sensory capability similar to vision. When in the body, the essence loses this capability due to interference from the organic matter; if the organic components of vision do not function, the essence cannot see. Once liberated from the body, however, the essence needs no organic substrate for vision (or its equivalent) and interacts with light directly. The theory thus *predicts* that blind near-death experiencers should experience visual perceptions during, and *only* during, their NDEs. At the end of the NDE, the essence returns to the body; if the body's visual system is impaired, then the essence will once again be blind. (Arnette, 1995c, p. 2)

In the case of Larry Dossey, it will be remembered, he took the trouble actually to contrive a *hypothetical* instance of a congenitally blind woman he named Sarah whose alleged NDE he described to start out his book, *Recovering the Soul* (1989) in dramatic fashion. He did so, of course, precisely because such an episode would be *logically* implied by his theory—such cases would *have to* exist if mind were truly nonlocal since "seeing" would not have to depend on an intact visual system. As he has his fictional mouthpiece, Sarah, say, "There's more than one way to see!" (pp. 18-19). And later, again speaking for Dossey, she is heard to muse, "My vision cannot be completely in my body ... and it cannot really all be in my eyes and my brain" (p. 19).

Amit Goswami, himself a theoretical physicist, has addressed OBEs and NDEs from the perspective of his theory in a paper, "Death and the Quantum" (1995a) and NDEs specifically in the blind in a special commentary and in correspondence with us. We focus here just on those implications of Goswami's theory for "seeing" during OBEs and NDEs. In this connection, however, it is important to note that Goswami posits a construct, which he calls "the quantum monad," that plays much the same role in his theory as the concept of "essence" does for Arnette. In Goswami's case, however, he is able to invoke such a construct without having to resort to the openly dualistic framework employed by Arnette. Goswami's language in what follows may *suggest* a form of dualism, but his theory is actually rigorously monistic throughout. In speculating about the role of the quantum monad in OBEs and NDEs, Goswami (1995a) raises this question:

> Is it possible to "be in" the quantum monad while living, while in our incarnate bodies? In out-of-the-body and near-death experiences people have autoscopic vision (vision of themselves) from a vantage point of hovering over their own body that can be explained as nonlocal seeing (through other people's eyes, the hovering surgeons). In these experiences, however, there is more than nonlocal

viewing. People who have these experiences report that they *were* out of their body, [and that] their identity *really* shifted from the usual physical body centered activity. To what? I think to one centered about the subtle body.... Clearly it is reasonable to assume that in these experiences people identify with their quantum monads, and with neither of the two correlated physical bodies involved. (p. 88)

In elaborating on these notions for us in his special commentary, Goswami (1995b) goes on to say:

The idealist science explanation [for "seeing" in the blind] is quantum nonlocality.... Explicitly, consciousness is collapsing similar states of perception in two locally separated brains that have become "correlated." Clearly, this way of "seeing" is available even if the subject is blind. (p. 1)

Because Michael Talbot died several years ago, we are forced to rely entirely on his last book, *The Holographic Universe* (1991) for his views on the possibility of "seeing" in the blind. In developing his own version of a wide-ranging holographic theory based largely on the previously articulated frameworks of such well-known theorists as David Bohm and Karl Pribram, Talbot makes it clear that visual perception in the blind during NDEs should be anticipated. And, for reasons similar to Dossey's, Talbot actually cites some of the anecdotal data from Kubler-Ross' work with her blind subjects, which we mentioned in our introduction, in an attempt to show that there were, at least in his judgment, already such data available (p. 242). Furthermore, in his discussion of OBEs as a holographic phenomenon (pp. 234-239), he also makes reference to some of the research on "eyeless sight," and concludes, "there is evidence that we too are not limited to seeing only through our physical eyes" (p. 237).

Finally, we come to the theoretical formulations of Jenny Wade who, like Talbot, was deeply influenced by Bohm's ideas and used them to undergird her own noetic theory of human development in her book, *Changes of Mind* (Wade, 1996a). Wade's theory, as will become evident, has many points of relevance to our data, and was expressly fashioned to deal with the phenomenology of the NDE in the context of her approach to the evolution of consciousness. She treats the NDE in general terms in one chapter of her book (pp. 223-247), but speaks to our research on the blind only in her special commentary from which we now quote the opening paragraph:

> I find your research on the blind compelling and—though not verifiable evidence for sight *per se*—certainly congruent with a theory such as mine which is couched in a holonomic paradigm that permits certain types of supraphenomenal experiences.... My theory is buttressed with evidence much like that you present, to wit, veridical accounts of extra-sensory impressions at times when the neurological system is severely compromised. Third-party corroborated impressions of "visual" images from the pre-natal and near-death literatures provide validated evidence of extra-sensory phenomena, including experiences typically characterized as visual, such as descriptions of distinctive colors and patterns in fabric, though the physiological basis for optical processing (eyeballs, optic nerves, visual cortex, etc.) may be entirely lacking. (Wade, 1996b, p. 1)

This passage, though it provides some evidence of Wade's sense of the congruence of our findings with her theory, is actually more fruitful than it may appear because it leads us directly to another domain of research that raises all the same theoretical questions as does our investigation of apparent sight in the blind. This concerns the study of another class of "impossible perceptions," namely those reported by adults of events they appear to have witnessed as infants *while still in utero* (e.g., Chamberlain, 1988; Cheek, 1986). Before we examine Wade's theory in more detail, let's take a moment to pursue this intriguing line of inquiry that forms such an obvious nexus to our own.

Consider first, for example, a couple of representative cases reported by perinatal researcher David Chamberlain. In a popular book Chamberlain (1988) wrote on the subject of apparent birth-related memories, he recounts a story that came from a three-and-a-half-year-old boy named Jason. Riding home one night, Jason spontaneously piped up that he remembered being born. He told his mother that he heard her crying and was doing everything he could to get out. It was "tight," he felt "wet," and he felt something around his neck and throat. In addition something hurt his head, and he remembered his face had been "scratched up."

Jason's mother said she had "never talked to him about the birth, never," but the facts were correct. The umbilical cord was wrapped around his neck, he was monitored via an electrode in his scalp, and was pulled out by forceps. The photo taken by the hospital shows scratches on his face (p. 103).

Another girl, not quite four, in speaking of her own birth, knew a "family secret" that had never been divulged to her. In this case, a friend of the mother and later an occasional babysitter named Cathy was present at the birth, assisting the midwife. After the birth, the midwife was busy and the mother had by then been helped into a bath, leaving Cathy temporarily alone with the baby. As the baby began to whimper, Cathy reflexively gave her to suck from her own breast. By the time the mother returned, the baby was already asleep, and Cathy, feeling somewhat guilty about being the first person to nurse the child, elected to say nothing to the mother about it.

Nearly four years later, Cathy was babysitting this same child, and, just out of curiosity, happened to ask the child if she remembered being born. As Chamberlain (1988) relates what Cathy later told him,

> She answered, "Yes!" and proceeded to give an accurate account of who was present and their roles during labor and delivery. She described the dim light of the womb and the pressures felt during birth. Then the child leaned up close and whispered in a confidential tone, "You held me and gave me titty when I cried and Mommy wasn't there." At that, she hopped up and went off to play. Says Cathy, "Nobody can tell me babies don't remember their birth!" (pp. 103-4)

Hearing such suggestive anecdotes as these, Chamberlain felt obliged to see whether he could confirm such reports through systematic research into the question. For this purpose, he eventually studied a paired set of ten mothers and children and independently hypnotized them, asking them for details about the birth from their separate perspectives. Of course, only mothers who could assure Chamberlain that they never shared details about the birth with their child were eligible for the study. For the purposes of evaluation, Chamberlain assumed that the report given by the mother would be at least an approximately accurate description of the circumstances of the birth against which the child's testimony could then be measured.

When comparing these independent accounts, Chamberlain (1988) found that in general the respective stories of mother and child agreed impressively, dovetailing on specific points of detail in an almost uncanny fashion. Here is how he summarizes his overall findings:

> Mother and child reports were coherent with each other, contained many facts that were consistent and connected, and were appropriately similar in setting, characters, and sequences. The independent narratives dovetailed at many points like one story told from two points of view.... Generally, reports validated each other in many details like time of day, locale, persons present, instruments used (suction, forceps, incubator) and type of delivery (feet or head first). Sequences of receiving bottled water, formula, or breast milk, appearance and disappearance of fathers, and moving in and out of different rooms were often consistent.... Considering all the facts, objectively gathered birth memories appear to be genuine recollections of experience. (pp. 106, 120)

Wade (1996b) herself, in her commentary, shows us the point of these comparisons:

> When regressed subjects are able to give accurate, detailed visual impressions of events that occurred while they were in utero—as independently validated by third parties—there can be little doubt that some extra-neurological, extra-sensory form of consciousness exists. Many of these impressions

have been dated to a time when the subject was, in fact, "doubly blind"—that is, unable to obtain visual inputs owing to its position inside the mother's body *and* owing to the fetal eyelids having still been fused. Even if, by some miracle, the barrier of the mother's body were removed, a hypothetical out-of-body fetus does not have even *remote* access to functional optical processing in its own body because the physical mechanisms for vision are too immature. Newborns can hardly see, never mind fetuses. The capability for optical processing remains very limited for full-term neonates. Contrast sensitivity and visual acuity are poor (perhaps only 20/600 Snellen) and newborns have difficulty focusing, fixating on stationary and moving objects, and even converging both eyes on a single target. It is difficult to see how the inchoate state of fetal neurological development would permit the accurate visual impressions obtained by a number of pre- and perinatal researchers.... [Thus], sensory processing, particularly vision, seems to function independent of the body's capabilities. (p. 1)

In short, what we have here is exactly the same conundrum we faced at the outset when confronted with reports suggesting that the blind might be able to see. As we have learned, it is not so much a matter of "seeing" as knowing, and it is of interest that Wade herself had independently arrived at a similar conclusion concerning her understanding of the nature of these pre- and perinatal impressions. Because her approach is so consistent with ours and her theory makes explicit reference to a number of the essential features suggested by our interpretation, including a highly articulated concept of transcendental awareness, we find her theoretical framework most helpful in explicating our findings here. Accordingly, in what follows, we shall present a few further selected aspects of Wade's formulation in an effort to sketch the outlines of a comprehensive and testable theory that can subsume, not only our data on the blind, but other similar anomalies as well.

Toward a theory of transcendental awareness: Some aspects of Wade's holonomic approach to nonlocal consciousness

Fundamental to Wade's thinking is a conception of human consciousness that is dual in nature. To begin with, there is of course a brain-based source of awareness which gives us our everyday experience of the world. But in addition, there is also what Wade calls "a physically transcendent source of awareness," which in her view—and her book offers a great deal of empirical evidence to suggest it—predates physical life and survives bodily death. The transcendent source of consciousness (TSC) is, she argues, particularly likely to be prominent in prenatal and near-death experiences, as well as in mystical states of consciousness, but tends to be damped out by brain-based consciousness during most of the life span. TSC, however, as already implied, is pre-existent and, as it were, "attaches itself" in an individualized form during the course of human life.

This implies that TSC has certain distinctive features, which are almost precisely those we have attributed to what we have called transcendental awareness. In this regard Wade (1996a) writes:

The physically transcendent source has its own form of awareness, whose maturity is not directly reflective of the level of the central nervous system functioning in the body. Its awareness is rather detached and highly insightful, but its phenomenology is inherently the world of dualism. It is capable of transcending physical limitations to some extent and of operating along with the brain-based consciousness.... Accessing the transcendent source permits experiences unbound by Newtonian spatiotemporality. (pp. 250-251)

This quotation makes it evident that although TSC allows the individual to experience nonlocal consciousness, that experience is often filtered through a template of dualism, as we have already noted. And elsewhere Wade insists that human beings come into this world wired with a dualistic spatiotemporal orientation that will remain with them through life and into death *unless* they have realized through spiritual practice or some other way a habitually nondualistic state of awareness. This is why she claims that TSC affords most persons only a *partial* release from a Newtonian world view, and in this connection points out that even the otherworldly visions in NDEs are typically dualistic in nature. This of course exactly mirrors the descriptions we ourselves have obtained from our blind respondents concerning their NDEs.

Nevertheless, Wade (1996b) suggests, even a partial escape from these built-in fetters of dualism seems to permit NDErs "to access a higher level of consciousness psychically, including having 'perfected'—or at least mature, undamaged—sensory experiences" (p. 3). In this respect, too, Wade's views parallel our own claimants' occasional indication that their perception in this state was "perfect" and thus in startling contrast to their usual apprehension of their environment.

In these ways, Wade's theory seeks to provide an encompassing framework in terms of which to explain the quasi-visual impressions of the blind we have examined at such length in this study as well as to help us understand the basis for other paradoxical and conventionally inexplicable findings, such as those based on pre- and perinatal research. To these further developments and applications we will look forward with a sense of confident expectation that they will represent important contributions to New Paradigm thinking.

Chapter Seven

A Concluding Word

When was not the science of the future
stirred to its conquering activities by the
little rebellious exceptions to the science of
the present?
                        -- William James

We began with an account of an NDE of a blind woman who afterward reported that she could see during her experience. At first blush, because this case was recounted by a well-known physician, we were probably inclined to take it at face-value, perhaps also influenced by our desire to believe in the miraculous. Almost immediately, however, we learned that the story that had so beguiled us into entertaining such an appealing possibility was bogus. But by the end of our inquiry, we came to understand that in this tale there resided still another paradox besides the one it seemed initially to represent—namely, that this was a story that was simultaneously true *and* false. Or perhaps we might better say it was a fictitious story that turned out to be true after all, just as the author all along had felt it just *had to be.* In this sense, at least, perhaps this author has received a measure of post-facto justification for his convictions, even if we cannot embrace, in this one instance, his penchant for prematurely converting belief into apparent fact.

Nevertheless, as we have seen, there is still another level of subtlety in this story because although in a sense it is true, it is not *entirely* true. The story of Sarah implies that she really could *see* during her NDE, in the way that a sighted person might. We have shown this is an unwarranted inference. What seems like an analog to physical sight is really something far more complex when examined closely. Rather it seems to be more akin to a distinctive and quite extraordinary mode of knowledge, which we have called mindsight. This mindsight, which seems to be a form of transcendental awareness, may yet be shown to function independently of the brain but must necessarily be filtered through it and through the medium of language as well. Thus, by the time these episodes come to our attention, they tend to speak in the language of vision, but the actual experiences themselves seem to be something rather different altogether and are not easily captured in any language of ordinary discourse. Indeed, our work has shown the need to exercise critical discernment before taking these reports at face value. To be sure, they make good stories, in books or in tabloid headlines, as the case may be, but they are not always necessarily what they seem.

What the blind experience is perhaps in some ways more astonishing even than the claim that they can see. Instead, they—like sighted persons who have had similar episodes—may have transcended brain-based consciousness altogether and, if that is so, their experiences will of necessity beggar all description or convenient labels. For these we need a new language altogether, as we need new theories from a new kind of science even to begin to comprehend them. Toward this end, the study of paradoxical and utterly anomalous experiences plays a vital role in furnishing the theorists of today the data they need to fashion the science of the twenty-first century. And that science of consciousness, like the new millennium itself, is surely already on the horizon.

Appendix

An Exceptional New Case of an NDE in the Blind

Just as this book was going to press, we learned of a new case of a blind NDEr, the details of which were, according to the account we read, quite astonishing with regard to the richness and clarity of the visual perceptions described by the NDEr. The case was originally reported on the web site of the Near-Death Experience Research Foundation (www.nderf.org) to which the interested reader is referred for further particulars about the NDEr in question.

When I (K.R.) first learned of this case, I was able to establish contact with the woman who had actually interviewed the NDEr, who, because she prefers to remain anonymous, I will simply call "Miss X" here. The interviewer was a psychologist, Tricia McGill, PhD., whom I had previously met and talked with at the 1998 conference of the International Association for Near-Death Studies. Dr. McGill kindly answered my many questions about the case and eventually arranged to put me in touch by phone directly with Miss X. It is only because of the kindness and permission of both Dr. McGill and Miss X that we can provide the information that follows regarding this remarkable case, including the bulk of the original report itself with which this appendix will close.

First, some background about this case is necessary to provide a context for the account we will present in a moment. Dr. McGill has informed us that after she learned the gist of Miss X's NDE, she was able to establish phone contact and very good rapport with Miss X. Over several weeks and many conversations, Miss X related her experience, which Dr. McGill taped. However, because her recording equipment was poor, Dr. McGill also took extensive written notes to supplement her tapes. The account you will read below reproduces Dr. McGill's transcription, which is based on all the information she gathered in this fashion from Miss X. She has told me that she believes that it is as accurate "as could be" under the circumstances and that it is "99.9% verbatim." Furthermore, once she had written up the report of the case but before she offered it on her web site, Dr. McGill sent it to Miss X to whom it was read by one of her roommates. After reviewing Dr. McGill's transcription, Miss X pronounced it accurate and gave Dr. McGill permission to present it on her web site.

After establishing that the report was, to the best of Dr. McGill's knowledge, accurate and virtually verbatim, I then asked her if she could vouch for the authenticity of Miss X's experience. Dr. McGill said unhesitatingly that she had no doubt about the matter and felt that Miss X had certainly had the experience she describes below.

Of course, as a researcher I was very keen to interview Miss X directly so that I could ask her some of the same probing and clarificatory questions we had put to our respondents in our study. Dr. McGill was perfectly willing to serve as go-between in this matter, but after speaking to Miss X regretfully told me this would not be possible. Here are the reasons. At the time I spoke with Dr. McGill about this matter (February 28, 1999), Miss X was quite ill and, understandably, was not in a position to entertain any questions from me. She was, however, willing to speak with me briefly on the phone, and so I did call her on February 28, 1999, and spoke with her for about ten minutes. She was polite, but told me that because of her medical circumstances, which she was forthright about, she simply was not up to being interviewed and that everything would have to go through Dr. McGill. However, I can attest that I do know this woman's name, phone number and where she lives—although, at her request, I can divulge none of that information here. A future meeting was not ruled out, but that would depend on her physical health and other factors. It will not occur in any case before the publication of this book.

Because of the undeniable relevance of this case, however, we decided that even though we cannot present it as one that we have investigated ourselves, it merited inclusion, without further comment or interpretation on our part, in an appendix. In effect, then, we offer it for its intrinsic value without being able to provide any external documentation of our own. In that connection, we must also state that the one person who might have provided some independent corroboration for some aspects of Miss X's NDE, her former landlady, died in 1998. What follows, then, is almost all of the original report on the NDERF web site. However, in deference to Miss X's explicit request, we cannot specify here the particular circumstances that brought her close to death. (For those details and for other information about this case, the interested reader is referred to Dr. McGill's web site.) What I am permitted to say in this connection, though, is that there was great pain involved and that, as Miss X's report makes clear, she was hospitalized for this condition, was comatose for three days, and, according to her physician, "it was a miracle" that she survived. For the rest of the story, we now turn directly to Miss X's own account, as painstakingly transcribed by Dr. McGill.

I have been blind since birth. Even as an adult, I lived with my parents until they died. They died suddenly in a car accident on February 14, 1994, Valentine's Day. I was devastated beyond words. I went into a severe depression and felt utterly alone and nearly helpless. If it weren't for my seeing-eye dog, Queenie, I would have felt abandoned completely. I owed my parents my whole world and my only friend was Queenie. When Queenie died of old age six months later, I was not sure if my life had any purpose or future.

My family and I were not religious, but I was born Jewish. Therefore, the thought of an after-life was considered to be merely wishful thinking. The rabbi had talked to me following my parents' death and offered very little comfort to ease my mental anguish. Nice, well meaning Jewish ladies would stop by periodically to bring me groceries and other things I needed, but it was clear that they felt slightly uncomfortable while visiting and after a few months their visits were very infrequent. I was too proud to accept help from strangers whom I was sure thought I was a moody burden. I knew that they felt sorry for me but didn't like me.

[Sometime after her parents' death, when Miss X was fifty, she found herself close to death and reports that] ... the pain was indescribable.... At the same time I could see for the first time. I was above my body looking at myself for the first time and feeling no love or even connection to it. The pain had stopped and I felt light and could move effortlessly. I thought as I was floating above my body that this was strange. I was feeling no pain and was thinking. The blank void I expected to find was not there. I was just drifting around the room and once again looked at myself below. I was shocked. I had never seen myself, of course, and thought I would be better looking. After studying my features very carefully for what seemed like an eternity, the thought suddenly hit me that if I could see myself, I could see other things too, and I thought what a wonderful, wonderful gift I was just given. WOW! Not only was I not in a dark void of nothingness, but I could actually see as well as think. Instead of imagining what my world (in the form of a tiny apartment) looked like, I could see it. Colors had been explained to me in terms of textures and smells, but nothing could have been said to prepare me for the reality of all those colors I was soaking in.

I then heard noises outside. There was somebody knocking on my apartment door. I thought to myself, "Well, I'd just go see who it is." I floated out into the hallway and saw that it was my landlady. I knew it was her, because she smelled like the cigarettes she smoked. She kept knocking on the door. I saw that she had a piece of paper in her hand and I was sure I knew that was my second eviction notice. I had no money to pay for the rent and I knew that I would have to be leaving soon. I studied her for a few seconds and then thought, "What am I doing here? I want to see the world!"

I soon floated right through the walls of the apartment building and was looking down on the street below. I saw people coming and going. I thought, "Well, let's go see if I can touch somebody." I floated down to a child that was on the street and I put my hand right through that child. I thought, "How odd. I can't touch them, but I still have a hand." I looked at my hand for a few minutes and noticed that it was glowing slightly and it was very transparent. I then scouted around looking at other things, until I went back to my body, seemingly drawn there by some unnatural force. I noticed that the landlady had let herself in and had discovered my body and was calling 911. "I don't want to be revived, I hope I'm dead because this is much better than life," I thought. I was floating around looking at various things in the apartment. The next thing I know there was this overwhelming sense of peace and love that just washed all over me. I hadn't felt this way since my parents were alive. I somehow found myself floating through a very brightly lit, oval shaped tunnel heading for a light that was way off in the distance. I felt no fear, only this pervading sense of peace and even some sort of wonderment. When I came out into the light I saw a man with a robe, beard and long brown hair. I said, "Who are you?" He telepathically communicated that his name was Jesus. "I don't believe in you," I said. He smiled and replied with the etheric equivalent of, "Well, I am here anyway!" Looking deeply into his eyes I asked, "Have you been with me all this time? Do you know me and care about me?" He grinned and seemed to be amused and said, "I have always loved you. Now, do you want to go or stay?" "Hey, give me a break," I yelled, only I made no sound, I just thought it. "I just died, I need a chance to get used to all this."

Suddenly, I was aware of a bright light that came directly up to me. The white light in front of me seemed to be giving off warmth. I remember thinking that my eyes should be burning but then, I remembered that I didn't have any earthly eyes to burn. This is what I thought a torch would look like, only more glowing and beautiful than words could describe. God was light and love and it was warm and it permeated every cell in my body. This was so wonderful, I was crying with a flood of tears that didn't exist. The light was so large, it was enormous, and I felt loved. I felt humble, amazed, and embarrassed by my flip attitude with His son. But most of all I felt even more completely, unconditionally forgiven and loved. Then I was suddenly zapped into a large room with square screens up and down the wall. There were dozens of, like, television screens. On each screen there was a movie of some event in my life: the good, the bad, the secret, the ugly, the uneventful and the special. Everything seemed to be going on at once. Nothing was in a particular order. It was silent. When you looked at the screen and you focused in, you could hear everything that was going on, not only in words, but your feelings and thoughts. Some of the screens showed me with Queenie and other dogs I've owned in the past. I realized that I could understand their thoughts too and how I affected their lives. I saw my parents and instantly recognized them as my parents. Even though I have never seen a picture of them I could tell immediately that they were my parents. In the screen I could see how I had been a blessing as well as a burden to them. I saw how much they sacrificed for me. I had kept them from doing many things they wanted to do for themselves. I was filled with a strong sense of responsibility to thank them for the constant care I had taken for granted.

"I gave you the precious gift of life," said the light. "What did you do with this gift?" I squirmed uncomfortably and said, in a weak voice, "Well, I'm blind, at least I was, I really didn't know I was supposed to do anything." "You can still accomplish much with your life," the light said, "Would you like to go back?" "To earth?" I questioned. "No way, why would I want to go back there? I want to stay with you." "Well, let me show you some things," said the light. The scene changed and I was no longer in that place.

I found myself in a meadow, a place of such beauty and peace that it made me gasp. This meadow had the most gorgeous, timeless, spaceless feeling to it. Being blind, I could only guess what grass, trees, mountains, clouds and streams look like. Now I was seeing it all!! It was the most incredible thing I had ever experienced. I was aware of delicate shifting colors with accompanying rainbows of gorgeous sound. The sound was like nothing I have ever heard on earth. It was like a series of chimes going up and down in pitch and volume in the most melodic way. I was curious where the music was coming from. I discovered that the music was born on the wind, the wind was creating the music. As the wind became stronger the music became louder. As the wind was fainter the music would die something like a wind chime. I was fascinated. I floated over a patch of wild flowers that were mostly yellow, bright purple and orange and they reacted to my presence by emitting a hum, which sounded like bells. I felt overwhelmed by the sheer beauty of it all.

The light being told me to look in a direction of a silvery stream. It shimmered in the sun. As I looked I could see two figures approaching. I didn't need to actually see these figures to know they were my father and my mother coming toward me. I seemed to dash off or fly into their presence in just under seconds. The time and space in this place didn't exist the way we know it on earth. Immediately my parents greeted me and I welcomed them with hugs and kisses. I couldn't believe that they were so real looking and so solid. I knew them by their personalities which was like a force they both radiated. They both were young and healthy looking. Before they died, dad was bent over and walked with a cane and both had glasses. They moved with grace and were fascinating to watch. The reunion was very touching. I never felt so deeply moved before. We communicated telepathically our love for each other and then my mom and dad both told me that it was so sad that I never accomplished much with my life. They felt that they didn't push me to do so because I never grew up in their minds. They never wanted their baby girl to experience any of the normal hardships of life because they felt in some way responsible for my condition. They both were over-protective of me during our lives together as a family. They had been shown that this had kept me totally dependent upon them and this was wrong.... It was important to them that I return to earth and finally complete the lesson on independence, which I had chosen prior to my birth.

At that point, the light being took over and communicated to me. I could either stay for a short time and then I would have to reincarnate and go through the same physical problems, such as blindness or some other handicap and suffer the deaths of loved ones and all the anxiety and depression that I experienced which had brought me right up to the point of my [death], along with the remainder of my life. Or, I could be sent back and finish out the rest of this life. I was told that I would be given certain gifts that would help me to deal with the situation and to have more of a successful life. The overall feeling that I got was terribly sad; I hadn't accomplished much with my life. I felt not so much guilt as I did a sense of responsibility, which I had avoided. Although I still felt totally loved, I sensed that all three of us had unknowingly played out our roles in this life in an uneventful way that hurt our individual self growth. Their devotion to meeting my needs kept them from having a life of their own and accomplishing things they dreamed of, and kept me from learning to do things on my own. I saw my cowardice ... rather than my taking responsibility for my life. I had been a fifty year old baby!

I asked a lot of questions about various things that cause people to have obstacles and problems in life and I got a lot of answers. I was told that we plan certain challenges to help us learn about life. I was shocked to learn that I chose blindness to learn a lesson of self-reliance and love. I was also told that before we are born, we have to agree that we will pretend and abide by the law of time and space, so that we can come here and advance in our spiritual growth and learning. If we don't agree to that, we can't be born. I learned that there were rules and order here in the after life.

I discovered the process of life and the acknowledgment and wonderment of each person's own unique abilities. I felt close to the reality of God's wonderful encompassing love. Before this I was not even sure that I believed in God, let alone Jesus. I was convinced that the idea of reincarnation was wishful thinking and that death was the end of our consciousness. I was told that God provides us with many opportunities for growth experiences during our lives. We have the free will to use, ignore or reject them.

I didn't realize before this time that I had some very serious issues of self-love, self-respect and self-validation and independence. I really needed to feel loved and accepted, but I was so sure that I would be rejected and looked upon as odd, just because of my blindness that I actually separated myself and isolated myself from the potential for a richer and more satisfying, happier life.

My fear of rejection was replaced with love and acceptance. I wanted to be the conduit of God's universal love. This love expanded to include all living things, not just other human beings. When that feeling was at its peak, a distant familiar bark alerted me to the presence of Queenie, my favorite and most loved of all my guide dogs. I instantly flew to her as she ran across a large field to get to me and we met. I fell down into the most luxurious, gorgeous grass as she licked my face and we reunited once again. I could sense her loneliness from having been separated from me and her joy at seeing me again. It was as if I could read her mind and she could read mine. It was incredible that animals have souls too. I never thought about it before. I suddenly knew that her mission in life was to help me. I wondered what my mission in life was.

Once again, I turned my attention to the being of light that was waiting patiently for me to get through with all of my thoughts and questions. I was told if I chose to go back that my parents and Queenie would be a daily part of my life and that other gifts would expand and open up to me. I was told that it was my job to learn what gifts I would be given. I said, "Yes, I'm ready to go back now." I said a fond farewell to my parents and Queenie. They left me one message: to love others and myself. I turned to search for the being of light, but he had already gone. The love that I felt in his presence remains with me until this day.

The next thing I knew I was hovering above my body as it lay in a hospital bed. Without particularly wanting to, I entered my body and it felt painful, heavy and very dense. I was readjusting to the feel of my body once again when a doctor entered the room. My eyes opened and I was hurt and disappointed, very disappointed, to find out that I was still as blind as ever. I was hoping that one of my gifts would be to keep my sight. It is so hard to go back to total blackness after seeing heaven. I recalled every insight I had been given and prayed to God and even Jesus to help me to be brave and accept all the challenges that lay ahead. The emotions finally got to me and I cried all the torrent of tears that I had felt like crying while in heaven, but they were not allowed there, I guess.

The doc immediately rushed over to me and began asking me questions. I was told later that I had been in a coma for three days. It was a miracle that I survived, according to the doctor. He had almost given up on me on a couple of occasions when my heart rate had slowed alarmingly. The nurses told me I was lucky to have cheated death…. I know, however, I had been spared to remember the lessons that my parents had given me to love myself and to love others. I knew that in order for me to develop the self-confidence I needed to do more with my life, I first needed to learn to love myself. I had to experience myself in a new way before others could. I knew the road was not going to be easy or fast, but it was a necessary part of what I had to do to learn my chosen lesson. This thought helped sustain me during the months of recovery. My former landlady turned out to be a nicer person than I knew. She visited me in the hospital four times, and was shocked when I told her that I had seen her efforts to save me. I described exactly what she looked like and the pink dress she wore the day I [died]. She believed me, and has been very helpful to me in the years that followed.

The gift that I was given apparently was an increased sensitivity to people's thoughts and feelings and a psychic ability which I had a little bit before my NDE, but it had increased a thousand times since returning. I am now making an adequate living as a psychic and have made many new friends. I've built up a self-esteem that I thought was impossible to do before. I am living with two other roommates whom I met through my eagerness to learn about my NDE and to develop my psychic gifts, and they are helping me with whatever I need that truly I cannot do for myself. With this newfound friendship, my life is now becoming more productive, independent and more joyful than I ever had dreamed would be possible.

One of the aftereffects of the NDE is that I do not automatically feel that I am unloved or unworthy. I feel that I have a contribution to make to society and I owe that to my NDE experience.

I was also shown after my life review that there really is meaning to our existence and that our handicaps were actually chosen by us before our earthly existence in order to help our progress towards a more spiritually developed soul.

I was considered to be a brave soul to take on that earthly challenge of being blind. I have had the good fortune to be able to astral project in my sleep, to visit with my parents and Queenie. They are proud of the lives I have touched with my psychic abilities, my growing independence and respect for my own worth. I know that even though I may not always be aware of their presence, they are with me in my daily life and are helping to guide me. I put a lot of stock in my intuition and feel it is my direct link to God and my parents who are my personal "angels." I was told that we only need to ask our angels and they will intervene and guide our lives. I have gone from being agnostic and bitter over my blindness and feeling helpless, to being interested in learning everything about how to use my gift to help spread the lessons of love to ourselves and to all others.

My grateful thanks to Dr. Tricia for her patience and effort to take down each word of this event in order to help provide inspiration to all.

Endnotes

1. This passage is from Grof's (1994) *Books of the dead*, p. 31.

2. This account is drawn from Larry Dossey's (1989) book, *Recovering the soul,* p. 17-19.

3. Other NDE researchers have independently discovered that this case was fabricated. See, for example, Susan Blackmore's (1993) book, *Dying to live*, pp. 131-132.

4. One of us (K.R.) remembers distinctly hearing such claims as early as 1981 at a meeting of the American Psychiatric Association in New Orleans.

5. Other investigators, not specifically identified with NDE research, even before Krishnan's appeal, had also advocated such studies. See, for example, Greenhouse (1975).

6. For example, see Susan Blackmore (1993), pp. 133-135.

7. Moody, personal communication, 1992.

8. We thank Fler Beaumont, an Australian researcher, for kindly bringing this and another of the following cases to our attention.

9. Jeffrey Iverson, (1992) *In search of the dead,* p. 68.

10. Kenneth L. Woodward, "There is life after death." *McCall's,* August, 1976, p. 136.

11. For example, in J. Kerby Anderson (1980), *Life, death & beyond* p. 91; and Gary R. Habermas and J.P. Moreland (1992), *Immortality: The other side of death*, p. 75.

12. Cited in I. Wilson (1987), *The after death experience,* p. 130. The last sentence of this quotation also appears, virtually unchanged, in Kubler-Ross' (1995) own book, *Death is of vital importance,* p. 72.

13. We would like to acknowledge Harry Cooper for bringing our attention to this case.

14. Irwin, 1987.

15. Krishnan, in commenting on Irwin's paper, also lamented that he had come up empty in his search for such cases. "For my part, I have so far not been able to find an instance of an OBE in a person born totally blind" (1987, p. 135).

16. Four of our respondents classified as blind from birth did have some limited light perception as children, but only two of these retained any as adults. Therefore, all but two of the persons in this category were without even any light perception at the time of their NDE or OBE.

17. The term, "visually impaired," simply denotes an individual with a recognized defect or malfunction of the eye. "Severely visually impaired" is a term used to refer to an individual who cannot read newsprint with prescriptive lenses. For a useful summary of the nomenclature of blindness and visual impairment, see J. Sardegna and T. Otis Paul (1991) pp. 30-33. However, it should be noted that we did not adhere strictly to this definition, since three of our visually impaired respondents could in fact read some print, although they could only do so with considerable effort and difficulty.

18. Legal blindness is defined as having corrected visual acuity in the better eye of 20/200 or less and/or a visual field in the better eye of 20 degrees or less.

19. Cases with complete names are used with the respondent's permission. If only a first name is given to identify a case for purposes of reference, it is a pseudonym.

20. Greg Wilson, an associate of Kimberly Clark Sharp of Seattle IANDS (International Association for

Near-Death Studies), conducted the initial series of interviews with Vicki for that organization.

21. One case, however, began with a frightening episode before it converted to the common radiant form.

22. Such comments recall the familiar remarks of Paul, "Now we see as in a glass darkly, but then we shall see face to face." (First Corinthians, 13:12)

23. Recently, we came across the case of an Australian woman—to be discussed later—who also reported seeing just an outline of her body when she was close to death.

24. Pat was interviewed four days before Cheryl.

25. It should be noted, by the way, that this witness had been separated from our participant for several years and they had not even communicated for at least a year before we interviewed him.

26. Super-ESP is the hypothesis that psi (e.g., extra sensory perception) is virtually without limits in accuracy and extension. This theory has been proposed by some parapsychologists as an alternative explanation to account for information purporting to come from deceased persons or discarnate spirits.

27. Romains' actual name was Louis Farigoule. He was born in 1885, studied both psychology and biology, and was also a novelist.

28. Recently, experiments by Yoichiro Sako and Tomoko Ono (1997) using two *soi-disant* "psychic" persons have provided corroborative evidence for a kind of non-visual dermal perception of colors, though the authors argue that clairvoyance may also be responsible for some of their findings.

29. Charles Tart has pointed out to us that whereas NDEs generally connote an altered state of consciousness, some ·OBEs, especially those "local"

episodes in which the individual is aware chiefly of being separated from his or her physical body, may actually involve a prosaically ordinary state of consciousness rather than the kind of transcendental awareness we are speaking of here.

30. Perhaps this is the place to make it clear that while this book of course concentrates on NDEs and OBEs, we do not mean to leave the impression that psi—or even eyeless vision—cannot occur in other contexts, some of which may not even involve altered states of consciousness as such. The exact relationship between such psi-mediated states and transcendent vision remains to be clarified.

31. For example, Ian Stevenson has kindly drawn our attention to a book, *The clairvoyant theory of perception*, written nearly fifty years ago, which can be used to illustrate this type of approach. There M. M. Moncrieff (1951) argued that ordinary vision is actually a form of clairvoyant perception. By his theory, the function of the visual system is to screen out a great mass of visual stimuli that would only overwhelm the individual and interfere with adaptive responses to the natural environment. However, in what Moncrieff calls higher forms of clairvoyance, the eyes are not involved at all and therefore "the perceptual knowledge acquired in these types of clairvoyance is independent of the visual sensory organs ... and would seem to transcend the physical and spatial conditions and processes associated ordinarily with visual perception (p. 42)." Although Moncrieff does not specifically mention blind persons in this connection, it is clear that his theory would have no difficulty in subsuming the general findings of this study.

References

Anderson, J. K. (1980). *Life, death and beyond.* Grand Rapids, MI: Zondervan.

Arnette, J. K. (1992). On the mind/body problem: The theory of essence. *Journal of Near-Death Studies, 11* (1), 5-18.

Arnette, J. K. (1995a). The theory of essence II. An electromagnetic-quantum mechanical model of interactionism. *Journal of Near-Death Studies, 14* (2), 77-99.

Arnette, J. K. (1995b). *A critique of pure materialism.* Unpublished masters thesis, Colorado State University, Fort Collins.

Arnette, J. K. (1995c*). A brief statement of the theory of essence.* Unpublished manuscript.

Atwater, P. M. H. (1988). *Coming back to life.* New York: Dodd Mead.

Audette, J. (1979). Denver cardiologist discloses findings after 18 years of near-death research. *Anabiosis, 1* (1), 1-2.

Bach-y-Rita, P. (1972). *Brain mechanisms in sensory substitution.* New York: Academic Press.

Bach-y-Rita, P., Scadden, L. A., & Collins, C. C. (1975). *Tactile television system.* San Francisco: Pacific Medical Center.

Blackmore, S. (1993). *Dying to live.* London: Grafton.

Chamberlain, D. B. (1988). *Babies remember birth.* Los Angeles: J. P. Tarcher.

Cheek, D. B. (1986). Prenatal and perinatal imprints: apparent prenatal consciousness as revealed by hypnosis. *Pre-and Peri-Natal Psychology Journal, 1* (2), 97-110.

Cook, T. H. (1970). *The use of visual concepts by blind and sighted children.* Unpublished doctoral dissertation, University of Houston, Texas.

Dillard, A. (1975). *Pilgrim at Tinker Creek.* New York: Bantam.

Dossey, L. (1989). *Recovering the soul.* New York: Bantam.

Duplessis, Y. (1975). The paranormal perception of color. *Parapsychological Monographs, 16.* New York: Parapsychology Foundation.

Goswami, A. (1993). *The self-aware universe.* Los Angeles: Tarcher/Putnam.

Goswami, A. (1994). *Science within consciousness.* Sausalito, CA: Institute of Noetic Sciences.

Goswami, A. (1995a). *Death and the quantum.* Unpublished manuscript, University of Oregon, Eugene, OR.

Goswami, A. (1995b). *Idealist science and the near-death experience.* Unpublished manuscript, University of Oregon, Eugene, OR.

Green, C. (1968). *Out-of-the-body experiences.* New York: Ballantine.

Greenhouse, H. B. (1975). *The astral journey.* Garden City, NY: Doubleday.

Gregory, R. L. (1966). *Eye and brain.* New York: McGraw-Hill.

Grinberg-Zylberbaum, J. (1983). Extraocular vision. *Psychoenergetics, 5,* 141-158.

Grof, S. (1994). *Books of the dead.* New York: Thames and Hudson.

Habermas, G. R., & Moreland, J. P. (1992). *Immortality: the other side of death.* Nashville, TN: Thomas Nelson, 1992.

Humphrey, N. (1993). *A history of the mind.* New York: HarperCollins.

Irwin, H. J. (1987). Out-of-body experiences in the blind. *Journal of Near-Death Studies, 6* (1), 53-60.

Irwin, H. J. (1987). *Flight of mind.* Metuchen, NJ: Scarecrow Press.

Iverson, J. (1992). *In search of the dead.* San Francisco: HarperSanFrancisco.

Kirtley, D. D. (1975). *The psychology of blindness.* Chicago: Nelson-Hall.

Krishnan, V. (1983). OBEs in the congenitally blind. *Vital Signs, 3* (3), 13.

Krishnan, V. (1987). OBEs in the blind. *Journal of Near-Death Studies, 7* (2), 134-139.

Kubler-Ross, E. (1983). *On children and death.* New York: Macmillan.

Kubler-Ross, E. (1995). *Death is of vital importance.* Barrytown, New York: Station Hill Press.

Liberman, J. (1995). *Take off your glasses and see.* New York: Crown.

Moncrieff, M. M. (1951). *The clairvoyant theory of perception.* London: Faber and Faber.

Moody, R. A., Jr. (1975). *Life after life.* Atlanta: Mockingbird Books.

Moody, R. A., Jr. (1988). *The light beyond.* New York: Bantam.

Newman, J. (1997). Putting the puzzle together. Part I: Towards a general theory of the neural correlates of consciousness. *Journal of Consciousness Studies, 4* (1), 47-66.

Nobbs, G. (1939, February). "I was blinded in Lousy Wood." *The Great War: I was there,* Part 20.

Poortman, J. J. (1978). *Vehicles of consciousness: The concept of hylic pluralism.* (Vol. 1). Wheaton, Illinois: Theosophical Publishing House.

Rathna, N. (1962). *A qualitative analysis of the visual terms used by the blind in their spoken language.* Unpublished doctoral dissertation, Indiana University, Terra Haute.

Ring, K. (1980). *Life at death.* New York: Coward, McCann and Geoghegan.

Ring, K. (1984). *Heading toward omega.* New York: Morrow.

Rogo, D. S. (1989). *The return from silence.* Wellingborough, England: Aquarian Press.

Romains, J. (1924). *Eyeless sight: A study of extra-retinal vision and the paroptic sense.* New York: G. P. Putnam's Sons.

Roszell, C. (1992). *The near-death experience.* Hudson, New York: Anthroposophic Press.

Sabom, M. B. (1982). *Recollections of death.* New York: Harper and Row.

Sacks, O. (1993, May 10). To see and not see. *The New Yorker.*

Sako, Y., & Homma, S. (1997). Clairvoyance and synesthesia. *Journal of International Society of Life Information Science, 15* (1), 169-172.

Sako, Y., & Ono, T. (1997). Non-visual color recognition. *Journal of International Society of Life Information Science, 15* (1), 36-49.

Sardegna, J., & Otis, T. P. (1991). *The encyclopedia of blindness and vision impairment.* New York: Facts on File.

Senden, M. von. (1960). *Space and sight.* New York: Free Press.

Steiner, R. (1989). *An outline of occult science.* (3rd ed.) Spring Valley, NY: Anthroposophic Press.

Steinpach, R. (1980). *How is it that we live after death and what is the meaning of life?* Stuttgart, Germany: Stiftung Gralsbotschaft.

Stoerig, P., Cowey, A., & Goebel, R. (1998). Blindsight and its neuronal basis. Consciousness research abstracts: Toward a Science of Consciousness 1998. Tucson, AZ: Consciousness Studies at the University of Arizona, 86.

Talbot, M. (1991). *The holographic universe.* New York: HarperCollins.

Valvo, A. (1971). *Sight restoration after long term blindness.* New York: American Foundation for the Blind.

Wade, J. (1996a). *Changes of mind.* Albany, NY: State University of New York Press.

Wade, J. (1996b). *Reflections on reports of visual impressions during NDEs in the blind.* Unpublished manuscript.

Weiskrantz, L. (1986). *Blindsight.* Oxford, England: Clarendon Press.

Weiskrantz, L. (1996, April). *Consciousness and commentaries: The role of extrastriate cortex in conscious vision.* Paper presented at Toward a Science of Consciousness conference, University of Arizona, Tucson, AZ.

Weiskrantz, L. (1997). *Consciousness lost and found.* Oxford, England: Oxford University Press.

Wilson, C. (1987). *Afterlife.* Garden City, NY: Doubleday.

Wilson, I. (1987). *The after death experience.* London: Sidgwick & Jackson.

Woodward, K. L. (1976, August). There is life after death. *McCalls.*

Yogananda, P. (1946/1972). *Autobiography of a yogi.* Los Angeles: Self-Realization Fellowship.

Index

214

The Institute of Transpersonal Psychology

The Institute of Transpersonal Psychology is a private, non-sectarian graduate school accredited by the Western Association of Schools and Colleges. The Institute's mission focuses on graduate education and research in the field of transpersonal psychology. The transpersonal orientation integrates consciousness studies, spiritual inquiry, body-mind relationships, and transformational aspects of human experiences into the study of psychology. Transpersonal experiences can have a profoundly transformative effect on individual lives and on society. These experiences often lead to development that transcends the conventional personal level and expands awareness beyond ordinary ways of perceiving, thinking, and feeling.

The Institute of Transpersonal Psychology supports a wide range of educational opportunities. Degrees offered support careers in education, research and business, and prepare students for state licensing as a psychologist or Marriage and Family Therapist. The institute offers on-campus masters and doctoral programs, and a Global Program presenting one-year certificates and masters programs in a distance learning format. The Institute offers an evening program for working adults and a unique on-line distance learning program which connects students from all over the world through the World Wide Web.

For more information on the Institute, contact: Institute of Transpersonal Psychology, Admissions Office, 744 San Antonio Rd., Palo Alto, CA, USA. Phone (650) 493-4430. You may also visit the Institute at: http://www.itp.edu or e-mail at: itpinfo@itp.edu.

The William James Center for Consciousness Studies

This book is published by the William James Center for Consciousness Studies. The Center is named after the eminent American psychologist and philosopher William James. His interests in consciousness, exceptional human experiences, psychic phenomena, education, healing, and spiritual experiences are continued in the field of transpersonal psychology today. The Center engages in research, publication, and activities that support a greater understanding of human consciousness, transpersonal human experiences, the process of transformation, and our nature as sensitive spiritual beings of vast and often unexplored potential. More information on the Center may be obtained from the WJCCS page on the ITP website at: http://www.itp.edu.